Writing Essays

A guide for students in English
and the humanities

Richard Marggraf Turley

London and New York

First published 2000 by RoutledgeFalmer
2 Park Square, Milton Park, Abingdon, Oxon, OX14 4RN

Simultaneously published in the USA and Canada
by RoutledgeFalmer
270 Madison Avenue, New York, NY 10016

Reprinted 2003, 2004, 2005, 2007, 2009

RoutledgeFalmer is an imprint of the Taylor & Francis Group, an Informa business

© 2000 Richard Marggraf Turley

Typeset in Sabon by
Keystroke, Jacaranda Lodge, Wolverhampton
Printed by the MPG Books Group
in the UK

British Library Cataloguing in Publication Data
A catalogue record for this book is available from the
British Library

Library of Congress Cataloguing in Publication Data
Marggraf Turley, Richard, 1970–
Writing essays : a guide for students in English and the humanities /
Richard Marggraf Turley.
    p.   cm.
Includes bibliographical references and index.
ISBN 0–415–23013–6
    1. English language—Rhetoric. 2. English philology—
Authorship. 3. Humanities—Authorship.
4. Criticism—Authorship. 5. Academic writing. 6. Report writing.
I. Title.

PE1408 .T87 2000
808'.042—dc21

00–029110

ISBN 978-0-415-23013-1

Writing Essays

Essays are an increasingly important form of assessment in higher education today, a fact which causes poor writers a great deal of anxiety and distress. Yet essay writing is simply a skill to be learned, like any other. Anyone can learn to express themselves coherently and unambiguously, and this book explains precisely how. If you are dissatisfied with your essay grades, or want to do better but don't know where to start, read on.

Writing Essays reveals the tricks of the trade, making your student life easier. You'll learn how to impress tutors with minimum effort by discovering exactly what markers look for when they read your work. Using practical examples selected from real student assignments, this book covers every aspect of composition, from introductions and conclusions, down to presentation and printing out. It also advises you on stress-free methods of revision, helps with exam essays, explains the principles of effective library management, shows you how to engage meaningfully with other critics' views, and introduces you to word-processing and the Internet.

As a full-time lecturer, Richard Marggraf Turley counsels students and assesses their work every day. His book recognizes the problems students face and addresses them directly and honestly, demystifying the whole process of composition. *Writing Essays* offers practical advice based on real-life writing situations, and is the ideal study aid, giving you confidence to improve your grades from the word go.

Richard Marggraf Turley is Lecturer in English at the University of Wales, Aberystwyth.

for Leah

Since every man whose soul is not a clod
Hath visions, and would speak, if he had loved,
And been well nurtured in his mother tongue.
John Keats
The Fall of Hyperion

Contents

Preface

For many students, 'essay' and 'nightmare' are virtual synonyms. That blank computer screen . . . the struggle for an idea . . . those first words! Perhaps the walls are closing in on you right now just thinking about it. But help is at hand. The written assignment is not an arcane branch of metaphysics, or an art that only the lucky few can master. Far from it. So long as a couple of rules are observed, much of the pain can be removed from the entire process of essay composition. This book tells you all you need to know about producing work that will impress even the most critical of readers. So no more late nights locked into the computer cluster, popping caffeine pills, weeping over your keyboard. A new day is about to dawn.

It is easy to appreciate why essay writing has destroyed thousands of autonomic nervous systems in colleges and universities. Current trends in higher education place an ever-increasing emphasis on the written assignment as a means of assessment, and many students find it difficult to cope. As a university lecturer, I see people practically every day who are terribly distressed because they simply don't know how to deliver what their tutors want from a piece of written work. The fact that the majority of students now pay for their education themselves means that not achieving the grades they need (or their parents expect) can lead to a sense of guilt, low self-esteem, and frustration. Some students even contemplate dropping out of their courses as a direct result of this pressure. Perhaps I am describing people whom you know. I could even be describing you, which might be why you are reading this book now.

After counselling some particularly stressed students earlier this year, I had the idea of composing a short guide to essay writing, which I duly distributed among members of my English Literature classes. The response was incredible: word quickly got around and before long I had students from other departments such as History and Philosophy queueing up at my door for a copy. Through interaction with these first readers, I was able to refine and hone my method. I also expanded the guide, making it more interdisciplinary, so that it now offers what I believe is the most relevant, rounded, up-to-date and accessible advice on essay writing available to students in college or at university (post-graduates working for MA or Ph.D. degrees should also benefit from reading it).

Unlike many study aids, mine works with examples taken from real essays and recent critical articles. In my opinion, an ounce of practice is worth a pound of precept: where other guides can waste precious time and space discussing hypothetical writing situations, I explain in concrete terms precisely what is good or bad about passages from genuine undergraduate work. Moreover, I show how to emulate what is impressive, and how to avoid doing what isn't. This 'hands-on' approach applies at every stage of the assign-ment – from introductions and transitions, to middle sections and conclusions. My book also gives you 'insider information' on improving style, organizing footnotes, using computers and the Internet, printing out, making the most of the library, revising for exams, and writing exam essays. And rather than asking you to plough through a thick tome, I keep everything strictly to the point, which means that I can be detailed and brief at the same time. Indeed, the keyword in my method is *accessibility*. If you have to study indexes to find the information you need from a guide, it has already failed. I've tried to make the learning process intuitive; if you are not drawn in as soon as you turn the first page, I want to know why!

This book is designed primarily for students of English and History, but will help anyone studying a range of humanities, including Anthropology, Archaeology, Philosophy, Geography, Media Studies, Art History, Cultural Studies, Music, and Education. In fact, a lot of what I have to say applies to essay writing in any discipline. Similarly, while my advice is aimed first and foremost at people working for a degree, adventurous A-level students will also find *Writing Essays* rewarding. I should clarify from the outset that this book will not *guarantee* you a first; nor will it magically transform you from a poor essay writer into a brilliant one. However, it will help you improve your writing skills substantially, let you into a few 'tricks of the trade', and get you thinking about the actual process of producing a coherent, grammatical, and above all *interesting* essay. Feel free to take or discard elements of what follows, according to what seems most useful or applicable to your needs. Above all, trust in your own abilities: when writing an essay – as with most things in life – there are many ways to skin a cat.

Finally, and to reiterate: the art of essay composition is not a jealously guarded secret, only revealed on full moons to the chosen few. It is merely a skill to be learned, like any other. A study guide that imparts this skill is a timely publication indeed, and writing it has not only been fun, but eminently worthwhile. The project belongs to an honourable and democratic tradition that can be traced back to William Cobbett's radical (and hugely popular) *Grammar of the English Language* (1818), which sought to teach a largely uneducated underclass of 'Soldiers, Sailors, Apprentices, and Plough-boys' how to express their meaning 'fully and clearly'. Cobbett's advice was as relevant then as it is now: 'The *only* use of words is *to cause our meaning to be clearly understood*.'

I've written this guide for you, and I hope you get a lot out of it. Your time at university or college should be fun, not a period of inordinate introspection and anxiety. Once you've realized this, the world, as they say, is your onion.

Richard Marggraf Turley

Acknowledgements

I would like to express my thanks to Anne Marggraf-Turley for the benefit of her thoughts and advice at various stages during this project. Thanks also to my parents, Krys and Dennis, and sisters Catherine, Anna, and Ruth. In any intellectual development, an individual receives nudges – or in some cases, two-handed shoves – from his or her fellow creatures. In addition to those already mentioned, I would like to acknowledge Damian Walford Davies, Richard Ebbs, Sandy Edgar, Katy Raine, Sandra Twitchit, Andrew and Alison Hadfield, Ed Carver, and Merel Noordenbos for their help along the way. I am indebted to my colleagues at Aberystwyth for providing a warm, mutually supportive, and inspiring working environment. I also wish to acknowledge former colleagues, mentors, and friends at Leeds, especially Andrew Wawn, Rory and Posy McTurk, John Whale, and John Barnard; and Peter Howbrook (for his early encouragement).

A special thank you to my editors at Routledge, Nina Stibbe and Jude Bowen, and to Maggie Lindsey-Jones, for their unflagging enthusiasm; and to all my students, past and present, from whom I've learned more than I care to admit. Oops, I just did!

I am grateful to Tim Woods, Claire Jowitt, Diane Watt, Anne Marggraf-Turley, Andrew Wawn, and Richard Ebbs for reading and commenting on early versions of chapters. I also wish to thank Catherine Michels, Rebecca Gray, Anna Turley, Katherine Bosley, Heather Stackhouse, Stuart Kime, Katy Raine, Jane Thomas, Andrew Michael, Michelle Begum, Edward Collins, Selima Davies, and Erika Mason, for allowing me to draw on their essays for examples. I hope I have not abused their trust.

Finally, my thanks are due to the following publishers for permission to use extracts from: John Nicholson, *Men and Women: How Different Are They?* (Oxford: Oxford University Press, 1984); Jeffrey N. Cox, *Poetry and Politics in the Cockney School* (Cambridge: Cambridge University Press, 1998); E. P. Thompson, *The Making of the English Working Class* (London: Victor Gollancz, 1968); Anthony Stevens and John Price, *Evolutionary Psychiatry: A New Beginning* (London: Routledge, 1996); Mary Evans, *Jane Austen and the State* (London: Routledge & Kegan Paul, 1987); Donna Haraway, *Simians, Cyborgs, and Women: The Reinvention of Nature* (New York: Routledge, 1991); and Donald J. Grout, *A History of Western Music*, 3rd edn (London: Dent, 1981). Thanks to the University of California Press for permission to quote from Scott McEathron, 'Wordsworth, *Lyrical Ballads*, and the Problem of Peasant Poetry', in *Nineteenth-Century Literature* 54 (1999), 1–26; to Edinburgh University Press for permission to quote from Thomas McFarland, 'Coleridge: Prescience, Tenacity and the Origin of Sociality', *Romanticism* 4.1 (1998), 40–59; to Blackwell Publishers for permission to cite David H. Close, 'Environmental Movements and the Emergence of Civil Society in Greece', *Australian Journal of Politics and History* 45 (1999), 52–64; to Routledge for permission to use Jane Moore's essay, 'Plagiarism with a Difference: Subjectivity in "Kubla Khan" and *Letters Written During a Short Residence in Sweden, Norway and Denmark*', in *Beyond Romanticism: New Approaches to Texts and Contexts 1780–1832*, ed. Stephen Copley and John Whale (London: Routledge, 1992); to the editors of *JAAC* for permission to use extracts from Nick Zangwill's article, 'Art and Audience', *Journal of Aesthetics and Art Criticism* 57 (1999), 315–32; to Harvester Wheatsheaf, for permission to cite Thomas Woodman, '"Wanting Nothing but the Laurel": Pope and the Idea of the Laureate Poet', in *Pope: New Contexts*, ed. David Fairer (Hemel Hempstead: Harvester Wheatsheaf, 1990); to CUP for allowing me to quote Susan Wolfson, 'Keats Enters History', in *Keats and History*, ed. Nicholas Roe (Cambridge: Cambridge University Press, 1995); and to Sage Publications for giving me permission to quote from Glenna Mathews, '"The Los Angeles of the North": San Jose's Transition from Fruit Capital to High-Tech Metropolis', *Journal of Urban History* 25 (1999), 459–76.

Chapter 1

How to write introductions

What do you want to say in your essay & why?

At school and university, various tutors will no doubt have given you different or even conflicting instructions on how to negotiate this crucial stage in your essay. Don't worry. This just underlines what I was saying in the preface about there being no single way to write essays. Besides, the best way of introducing an essay often depends on what it is you have been asked to write about. But a tried and tested method is that which gives the reader a clear, unambiguous statement of aims. That is, tell the reader *what* you intend to talk about, and most importantly *why*. A good example of an essay that does exactly this is Jane Moore's 'Plagiarism with a Difference: Subjectivity in "Kubla Khan" and *Letters Written During a Short Residence in Sweden, Norway and Denmark*', in *Beyond Romanticism*, ed. Stephen Copley and John Whale (London: Routledge, 1992). This is Moore's first paragraph (don't worry about the technical terms; just concentrate on how the paragraph is organized):

> In 1927 John Livingston Lowes alleged that parts of Mary Wollstonecraft's *Letters Written during a Short Residence in Sweden, Norway and Denmark*, published in 1796, quietly reappear in Coleridge's 'Kubla Khan', which was written the following year (Lowes 1978: 148, 545). Lowes's suggestion has set the agenda for much later discussion. My own paper, written from the theoretical perspectives of feminist post-structuralism and Lacanian psychoanalysis, places Coleridge's plagiarism within the field of sexual politics and the politics of desire and power as they are played out in Romantic writing. I propose the thesis that the plagiarism of *A Short Residence* can be read as an attempt by the male Romantic, Coleridge, to fill in the lack which Lacan argues is the condition of subjectivity.

> (p. 140)

This is great – in a short space, Moore not only sketches a critical context for Wollstonecraft's *A Short Residence*, moreover one that is specific to the themes she wants to discuss in her own essay; she also tells us what her approach is (feminist poststructuralism and Lacanian psychoanalysis), and what her essay adds to the debate on Wollstonecraft. In a few deft moves, Moore informs her reader and engages his or her attention with the promise of an interesting discussion. By making her aims and objectives clear, she also gives her reader a map or compass by which to navigate the rest of the essay. Moore hasn't kept back her best point as some 'prize' for the assiduous reader to discover; she hasn't treated her essay like a detective novel, where the 'solution' is withheld until the last page. Rather, she uses a direct and economical mode of address to communicate from the outset all the information the reader needs to get the most out of the essay.

The introduction is all about setting out your stall – about letting your reader know what to expect, and telling him or her where you are coming from critically. So, let's do just that. Assume we've been asked to write on images of solitude in Wordsworth's and Coleridge's poetry. We'll use 'Simon Lee', 'The Ancient Mariner', and 'Resolution and Independence' as our texts, and work up a thesis that solitary figures are intimately associated with rapid social change, anxiety, and alienation in the late eighteenth century (again, don't worry if you don't know the poems; just focus on how I organize my ideas). OK, we know what we want to say; now all we have to do is say it:

> In 1798 Samuel Taylor Coleridge and William Wordsworth published *Lyrical Ballads*, a volume of poems that eschewed 'lofty' neoclassical themes in favour of situations drawn from the lives of labourers, idiot boys, and vagrants. *Lyrical Ballads* appeared at a time of intense and rapid social change in which traditional jobs and ways of life vanished; seemingly overnight, many people became virtual anachronisms in their own age. This essay explores Wordsworth's and Coleridge's interest in solitary figures such as the Leech Gatherer in 'Resolution and Independence', the Ancient Mariner, and Simon Lee, and suggests that for these poets solitary figures are striking emblems of alienation and disempowerment.

Well, this introduction might not win awards, and would be much improved if I could find a quote from a literary historian corroborating my view of the frightening pace of social change in the late eighteenth century. But that notwithstanding, in the passage I tell the reader what my essay seeks to do, make clear my interest in relating literature to the historical period that produced it, and manage to come up with one or two nice turns of phrase (I quite like 'solitary figures are striking emblems of alienation and disempowerment'!).

Internal coherency

Read through the paragraph again. Notice how one point moves smoothly and elegantly into the next, in a logical sequence.

This sequence, if broken down into units, looks something like this:

1 *Lyrical Ballads* differed from previous volumes of poetry by placing new emphasis on 'lowly' characters such as labourers and vagrants.

→ 2 Text appeared at an historical juncture characterized by rapid social change, when many traditional jobs and ways of life were disappearing.

→ 3 Essay focuses specifically on how Wordsworth and Coleridge use solitary figures to explore the plight of those left stranded in those uncertain times.

If the order of the units were rearranged, the introduction would no longer be as effective. Actually, it is a good idea to apply this 'internal coherency' test to your own introductions. I'll be looking at another example of this a little later on.

Useful phrases

One more thing to note. In the last sentence of my introduction, I've used a simple and very convenient phrase for outlining the scope of my essay:

This essay explores . . .

Other ways of saying the same thing are:

In this essay, I want to investigate/consider/detail . . .
This essay examines/demonstrates/contends/proposes that . . .
This essay seeks to determine . . .
This essay will concentrate on . . .
My discussion draws into focus . . .

When you come across pithy phrases or expressions in the work of good critics, don't be afraid to 'lift' them for your own use. The chances are that the phrase in question has already been adapted from someone else. Don't lift *ideas*, though. That's plagiarism, and you'll go to prison for it.

By the same token, there are certain phrases or formulas that it is best to avoid as you would the plague. For example:

> In order to respond to the question, it is first necessary to examine Dudley's position in the Elizabethan court.

I'm sure you all recognize the *in order to do X, it is first necessary to do Y* formula. It probably seems like an old friend who is always there for you. But, while it may be a mainstay of sixth-form essays, it has no place in undergraduate work. It is too clunky, predictable, and obviously 'A-levelly'. As soon as you fall back on it, the words **'No imagination!'** will start to flash in your tutor's mind in thirty-foot-tall neon letters.

Express yourself

Before we move on, I want to look at one more 'exemplary' introduction to demonstrate that what we have been discussing applies not only to English Literature essays, but counts equally in other areas of the humanities. My last example is taken from an article by Glenna Mathews, entitled '"The Los Angeles of the North": San Jose's Transition from Fruit Capital to High-Tech Metropolis'. It appeared in *Journal of Urban History* 25/4 (1999), 459–76:

> Before World War II, San Jose, surrounded by the fertile and orchard-filled Santa Clara Valley, was the undoubted capital of fruit growing and fruit processing in the United States. Indeed, as late as 1960, there were still 215 food-processing operations in the Valley of Heart's Delight – so-called because of its scenic splendour during blossom time. But by that time, the area was well on the way to becoming Silicon Valley. This essay will first address the process of change in general, and then focus on two areas of public policy, water and schools, that were essential to the transformation and that offer contrasting scenarios in terms

of their resolution. Examined together, they cast in bold relief the tensions between the forces of consolidation and those leading to fragmentation in post-war American cities.

You'll recognize several elements essential for a good introduction in this passage. There is an unambiguous statement of aims outlining the scope of the discussion ('this essay will first . . . and then . . .'), the grammar is clear throughout, and ideas progress logically. In addition, the prose style is simple but stylish, and there is no disfiguring jargon (the 1980s spawned articles full of vapid expressions like 'ideological hermeneutics', 'dialectical negotiation', and 'the dialogics of desire'. Do not be tempted to emulate!). I also like the way Mathews finds a few finely turned phrases, such as 'cast in bold relief . . .', to lend definition to her points. She has obviously given the matter of composition some thought – as you should – and produces one or two wonderfully evocative images, such as the 'fertile and orchard-filled Santa Clara Valley'. These deft touches help win the reader over, or 'enlist' them, as the Americans say.

A good first paragraph is all about striking the right note, or, to switch metaphors, giving your reader a firm handshake. After all, as the word suggests, an introduction introduces you to someone for the first time. Don't make your reader feel like he or she has just squeezed an uncooked sausage. Remember, it pays to think carefully about your introduction, because from it your reader forms a first impression of you. And as Martin Chuzzlewit reminds us in Dickens's novel of that name: 'First impressions, you know, often go a long way, and last a long time.'

More on sequential logic & saying what you mean

It is time to turn to a real student essay from a third-year English undergraduate, whom we'll call Dan, although all names in this book have been changed to protect the guilty. By now you should be able to spot what's hot about Dan's introduction, and what's not. His essay discusses Jane Austen's *Sense and Sensibility*, and begins like this:

Marriage in Austen's society was perceived as a functional device far removed from any emotional rhetoric. Marriage was a, 'Social and material contract,' (Evans p46) in which emotion should be subordinated and kept firmly under control. From a purely personal point of view Austen herself proved that a woman, could be, 'Capable of acting independently of men and patriarchal interests.' (Evans p44) I will argue however that this notion was not practical to most of the women in Austen's society and certainly remains largely impractical to the protagonists of "Sense and Sensibility".

A lot of things are done well here, although by no means everything. For instance, we ought to clarify (as it seems to have slipped Dan's mind) that the critical reference to Mary Evans is to her book, *Jane Austen and the State* (London: Routledge & Kegan Paul, 1987). Since Dan quotes from this publication for the first time, a full bibliographical reference needs to go in a footnote (more on this topic in chapter 7).

Let's look at the passage in more detail now. We can start by rectifying the careless slips in punctuation. Compare the above with the 'tidied-up' version that follows:

Marriage in Austen's society was perceived as a functional device far removed from any emotional rhetoric. Marriage was a 'social and material contract' (Evans, p. 46), in which emotion should be subordinated and kept firmly under control. From a purely personal point of view, Austen herself proved that a woman could be 'capable of acting independently of men and patriarchal interests' (Evans, p. 44). I will argue, however, that this notion was not practical to most of the women in Austen's society, and certainly remains largely impractical to the protagonists of *Sense and Sensibility*.

See how the flow of the essay has been improved merely by moving a few commas around? Not a single one remains where Dan originally put it. When you read your essays through, don't just scan for spelling mistakes and awkward expressions, but also for any odd punctuation that will make your tutor's task more gruelling than it need be. I'll look closely at grammar and punctuation in Chapter 5, but for the moment I want to draw your attention to one very simple rule: *never* put commas immediately before round brackets. I don't care who told you to do it – it is pernicious and evil. You must stop it now and for all time.

Let us take another look at the revised paragraph. Notice how I have altered the page references to Evans's book (see Chapter 7 for a full discussion of this subject). As it stands, 'p46' looks awful. The 'p' is jammed up awkwardly against '46' to produce an ugly jumble of characters. By inserting a full stop and a space, we create a clearer, visually more appealing reference. After all, we should not only be aiming for grammatical clarity and perspicuity in our essays, but also for *visual* perspicuity. An essay is a physical object, and the reader cannot help but be influenced by its appearance. If you have printed yours out on lavatory paper (assuming you've printed it out at all), in minuscule type, without spell-checking or proof-reading it, then your tutor will probably assume that as little thought has gone into what it has to say as into its presentation. Because student numbers have exploded in recent years, tutors no longer have time (or the inclination) to decipher tatty, badly presented essays. If you want yours to receive proper attention, make sure it is well presented and easy to read. You will be repaid for your trouble with better marks.

Back to Dan. I said that some things had been done well: there are a couple of quotes, a section locating the discussion within the critical debate, and a sentence telling the reader what his essay seeks to establish. But things could still be improved.

Let's look at each sentence in turn:

(1) Marriage in Austen's society was perceived as a functional device far removed from any emotional rhetoric.

Apart from the rather sweeping statement about marriage in the late eighteenth century, and the flaccid passive construction (I'd like to know *who* is doing the perceiving), this sentence is quite promising. At any rate, we have two quite nice phrases in 'functional device' and 'emotional rhetoric'. However, I wonder whether we have sacrificed clarity for a clever turn of phrase, which is never a good trade-off. Does it really make sense to say that marriage is a 'functional device'? For that matter, what *is* a 'functional device'? What Dan means, but doesn't quite say, is that *financial security, rather than emotional attachment, was often the most important reason for getting married in Austen's society.*

Your reader shouldn't have to think around several corners to arrive at the sense of your argument. Be absolutely clear in your own mind what you want to say. Then, and only then, work out the best way of saying it. Finally, check that what you've written reflects what you wanted to say. It sounds obvious, but how many of you actually do this?

We'll move on to the second sentence:

(2) Marriage was a 'social and material contract' (Evans, p. 46), in which emotion should be subordinated and kept firmly under control.

This isn't *too* bad. It just needs a little re-jigging to avoid an awkward use of 'should be'. We could change this to 'was' or 'had to be'. The third sentence, however, presents more of a dilemma:

(3) From a purely personal point of view, Austen herself proved that a woman could be 'capable of acting independently of men and patriarchal interests' (Evans, p. 44).

Here we have a problem with 'sequential' logic – both within the sentence itself, and in the sentence's relationship to the paragraph as a whole. If we were to break the paragraph down into units, as we did with mine earlier, we would end up with the following:

1 No automatic connection between love and marriage in Austen's day.
→ 2 Evans's quote that women could in fact live independently from patriarchal interests.
→ 3 Austen's life itself proves this.
→ 4 But novel seems to suggest that the opposite was true.

Something is wrong. *How* does Austen's life prove that women could live without being fettered to patriarchal interests? We appear to be missing a crucial piece of information, namely that Austen did not marry. Unless the reader happens to be familiar with the details of Austen's biography, Dan's point just doesn't make sense. In other words, we need to add to the sequence the fact that Austen never married:

  1 No automatic connection between love and marriage in Austen's day.
→ 2 Evans's quote that women could in fact live independently from patriarchal interests.
→ 3 Mention the fact that Austen did not marry.
→ 4 Austen's life thus proves Evans's point.
→ 5 But her novel seems to suggest that the opposite was true.

That's better!

We'll continue our scrutiny of Dan's introduction. We're still on the third sentence and considering the matter of coherence, this time *within* the sentence. Can we really say that '*From a purely personal point of view*, Austen herself proved that a woman could be "capable of acting independently of men and patriarchal interests"'? Er . . . no. This is desperate, Dan. But I think I can see what has happened. Dan has mixed up what he *wanted* to say – 'from the point of view of her personal life' – with a similar-sounding expression: 'a personal point of view'. Of course, Austen's *personal point of view* has nothing to do with proving whether or not women can live independently from men. But if we consider the proposition *from the point of view of her personal life*, then things start to fall into place.

Right, last sentence:

(4) I will argue, however, that this notion was not practical to most of the women in Austen's society, and certainly remains largely impractical to the protagonists of *Sense and Sensibility*.

It is not clear to me what 'this notion' is supposed to signify. I can see that it must have something to do with Evans's contention that women were capable of operating independently from men, but things are a little confusing, aren't they? This is because 'notion' is the wrong word to use. 'Notions' are neither practical nor impractical (whereas, say, 'suggestions' *are*). By 'this notion', Dan actually means 'this way of living' (i.e. independently from patriarchal interests), which indeed was not practical for many women.

If we wanted to keep this sentence, we would have to rewrite it thus:

> As I will argue, however, living independently from men was not always practical for women in Austen's society, and certainly remains . . .

You can see how making your words say exactly what you intend takes a bit of effort. It is by no means impossible – you just have to be aware that meaning has a tendency to 'slip its leash' if you don't keep a firm grip on it.

Putting it all together

To bring this chapter to a close, let's have another go at Dan's introduction, paying attention to all the points that have been raised:

> In Jane Austen's society, marriage often had less to do with emotional attachment than with financial security. Indeed, Mary Evans notes that marriage was first and foremost a 'social and material contract', in which the emotions were kept firmly under control.[1st REF IN FOOTNOTE] But, as Evans also points out, women were, in principle at least, 'capable of acting independently of men and patriarchal interests' (p. 44). The fact that Austen did not marry would seem to bear this out. Yet the experiences of the female protagonists in *Sense and Sensibility* suggest that, on the contrary, independence was far from practical for most women. In the following discussion, I want to contend that Jane Austen's life and art present the modern reader with an intriguing contradiction.

This is a lot better. There might still be a few question marks hanging around, but these are now confined to how far one agrees with Dan's thesis, rather than centring on issues of basic comprehension. Arguably, choosing two contradictory quotes from the same critic is not the best policy, and at times it is slightly unclear who is arguing against whom in the above passage. I have had to add 'in principle at least' in the third sentence to try to get around this predicament. But at least now the reader is able to engage with what promises to be a stimulating discussion, rather than having to work out what Dan means.

And writing an introduction is as simple as that.

Note:

1 Say **what** you want to talk about and **why** (aims of essay).
2 **Locate** your argument in the critical debate.
3 Check that your ideas progress in a **logical** sequence.
4 Make sure that you always **say** what you **mean**.

Chapter 2

The middle section: structure & critics

The middle section is where you make good the promises of your introduction. No matter how virtuosic, well-written, and internally logical your opening paragraph is, in the middle section you have to *deliver*. As with all areas of essay composition, there are things to do and things to don't, and once you know what these are you'll feel a lot happier. So read on, Macduff!

I have divided 'The middle section' into two chapters. The first looks at *structure*, and shows you how to organize your thoughts into an intellectually mobile and energetic argument. I'm also going to talk in this chapter about how and when to use critics (even, or rather *especially*, when their views contradict your own). The second, on *linkage*, is concerned with movement within this larger structure, and explains how to progress smoothly between sentences, paragraphs, and sections.

Reading the question & structuring your argument

Let me begin by saying that a good essay has to have a good structure. Sorry to be prescriptive all of a sudden, but this rule affords no exceptions. If you don't think about structure, you will almost certainly end up with a sprawling, lurching, sporadic argument, that will neither convince nor persuade, and will most likely exasperate your tutor to the point of distraction. Although most people do not realize it, structural problems usually start not with the essay, but with the question. People dive in without making absolutely sure they know precisely what it is they have been asked to do. They seize a few key terms and head off into what they think is the sunlight, but which frequently turns out to be the headlamps of an oncoming juggernaut.

Spend more time on the question, because it will point you towards the most felicitous way of organizing the essay. Let's explore this idea with the aid of a typical humanities essay question. It asks us to discuss a poetic genre called 'dramatic monologue':

> 'The Victorian dramatic monologue, as exemplified by Tennyson and Browning, involves a retreat from the Romantic "I" into the mask of persona.' Discuss.

The format will probably be horribly familiar to you. There is an unacknowledged quotation, followed by an ominous invitation to 'discuss'. 'Discuss what?' – 'Help!' – 'Medic!' But there's really no reason to panic. The question, if it is any good, will possess a clear, logical internal structure that 'resonates' at a particular frequency. By listening carefully, you can find a structure that compliments it. Of course, there isn't only one 'correct' way to arrange your thoughts into an essay on 'dramatic monologues'; but it's much easier to work with a structure that is in harmony with the question, rather than in disharmony.

What structure does our question on dramatic monologues suggest to us, then? What frequency is it resonating at? Before we can answer this, we should look at one of those tricky words from the question in more detail. What on earth is meant by a 'dramatic monologue'? In the hands of Victorian poets Alfred Tennyson and Robert Browning, it is a poem written from a first-person perspective (e.g. 'I wither in thine arms', from Tennyson's poem 'Tithonus'), where the 'I' is not (on first glance, at least) the author, but a persona, usually a mythical or historical figure. So in 'Tithonus', the 'I' who speaks is not Tennyson, but rather the mythological personage named in the title of the poem. Let us remind ourselves of our task:

> 'The Victorian dramatic monologue, as exemplified by Tennyson and Browning, involves a retreat from the Romantic "I" into the mask of persona.' Discuss.

Listen carefully. Can you hear that, for all the technical terms, the question has a very simple A–B structure. It merely invites us to compare (A) Romantic first-person poems with (B) Victorian ones (i.e. 'as exemplified by Tennyson and Browning'). Don't be fooled by the fact that Tennyson and Browning appear before the reference to Romantic poems; think in terms of chronology, since essentially all we are being asked to do is consider a chronological progression from 'I' poems of the Romantic period of 1790–1820 to 'I' poems of the early Victorian period of the 1830s and 1840s. It would make no sense at all if we were to look first at Tennyson's and Browning's use of 'I', and *then* go back to see what was different about their forerunners. This would stress the Romantic part of the question, whereas our emphasis should be firmly on the Victorians, Tennyson and Browning (who are, after all, the named writers in the question). In other words, we should begin by looking briefly at a few first-person Romantic poems, and then see what was different about those written by Tennyson and Browning. The question even tells us what particular aspect of difference we should focus on: the use of the persona as a 'mask'.

This isn't meant to be a lecture on Victorian poetry, so I won't bore you by saying that the Romantic poet asks to be identified with the 'I' of poems such as Wordsworth's 'I wandered lonely as a cloud' or Percy Shelley's 'I fall upon the thorns of life! I bleed!'

(the more personal and 'genuine' the experience being recounted, the more 'Romantic' the poem). I also won't try your patience by explaining that, by contrast, Tennyson can't risk being identified too closely with the 'I' of *his* first-person monologues, since these poems often dramatize sensitive issues such as same-sex love (Tennyson – to the despair of his father – doted on his friend Arthur Hallam). And I won't even venture to outline how, by hiding behind persona in the dramatic monologue, Tennyson finds a way to express his love for Hallam publicly, while protecting his reputation in a censorious age.

All I *will* say is that the middle section of an essay answering the above question on Tennyson and Browning could profitably adopt the following broad structure:

A. Discuss Romantic first-person perspective ('I') poems, drawing attention to some defining features.

B. Discuss a couple of 'I' poems by Tennyson and Browning, explaining how and why these writers departed from the Romantic tradition they inherited.

Within this framework there will be plenty of room for incorporating critical opinion (as I will illustrate in a moment or two), for agreeing or disagreeing with the question, and for providing an alternative theory of dramatic monologue. One might, for example, want to take issue with the notion that the transition from a Romantic 'I' to a Victorian 'I' constitutes a 'retreat'; alternatively, one might wish to challenge the idea that the persona acts as a mask for the author. Whatever the case, our broad A–B structure, as suggested by the question itself, remains an accommodating frame within which to explore the terms and scope of the question. 'Finding' this structure won't make the essay write itself, but it will help you to write it with greater ease.

Using critics

Some students consider it a point of honour to write all their essays without the assistance of a single critic. Whether this is due to a misplaced faith in their own abilities, or sheer delinquency, I'm never quite sure. But whatever the case, the only losers are the students in question. Not only do they sacrifice the chance to encounter new ideas from people working at the forefront of their respective fields. On a more pragmatic level, they also forfeit an opportunity to develop their vocabulary, style, and argumentative skills. 'No man is an island', said John Donne. This is patently true in the sense that one would be hard-pressed to push someone out to sea and live on them. But it is also true in the sense that we need each other's views and opinions in order to develop our own. If you fail to interact with other people's notions when you write, your work will become introspective and incestuous. On the other hand, read an interesting work of criticism and suddenly your thoughts will meet gratefully with others, hold hands, form playful alliances, multiply brightly . . . flashing . . . gleam . . . gleam . . . whoosh! Well, I'd better leave it there before they come to wheel me off. On a more serious note, though, if you don't read criticism you won't know the difference between an original idea and 'old hat'. If you really want to spend hours re-inventing the wheel, go ahead. Just don't expect your tutor to be impressed.

Most institutions print lists of criteria an essay has to satisfy to attain a certain grade. I'm willing to go out on a limb and wager that practically every list in the country includes 'evidence of engagement with the critical debate', or some such formulation, as one of the criteria for an essay of 2,i standard or higher. In layperson's terms: read around your subject.

Now that we've established *why* we use criticism, let's turn our attention to *how* we use it.

The first thing to say is that you should not allow your ideas to be swamped by other people's. There is nothing worse than an essay that lollops from one critical summary to another, before adding 'I agree with X' and promptly keeling over. Critics are there for four reasons, and in each case *you* should be in control:

1 to provide support or authorization at crucial points in your argument
2 to be disagreed with as a means of developing your material
3 to act as sounding boards for your ideas
4 to act as springboards for your ideas

The critic as support

Let's look at some examples of each kind of usage. We'll begin with using the critic to shore up your own argument:

> The full extent to which the Internet threatens to impact, or is already impacting, on modern life, is only just beginning to become clear. As Michael Jones points out in *The Internet and I* (Bangor: Spinner, 1999), 'in the last three years the number of computers in western households has increased ten-fold, a figure matched only by the number of modems sold during the same period' (p. 46).

You can see that I have merely used Jones's statistical research to underpin my own thoughts on the likely influence of the Internet. I am in control.

Disagreeing with critics

A point of critical contention can be used to open up a discussion helpfully. Moreover, if you can disagree convincingly with an 'expert', your tutor will see that you have reached an advanced stage in your understanding of a particular topic. Take a look at the following passage:

> In his recent article '"Strange Longings": Keats and Feet', in *Studies in Romanticism*, Richard Marggraf Turley takes cynical, directed (mis)readings of theory, in this case Freudian, to ludicrous extremes. To say that Keats's sexuality was 'boyish' is one thing; to say that a key figure in British cultural heritage was a foot fetishist is quite another. Evidently, Marggraf

Turley's thesis is intended to be a joke, but it is a bad one. The problem lies in a patent misunderstanding of Keats's own sense of humour, which, as we see at work in a playful letter to John Hamilton Reynolds, is . . .

Oooh! That hurt! But the point to take is that 'outraged from Tunbridge Wells' has used resistance to my view of Keats to open up and develop their own discussion of the poet's humour. And when I find out where he or she lives . . .

The critic as 'sounding board'

By 'sounding board', I mean something against which you can test your ideas until you arrive at a satisfactory intellectual position. It can be fun to let the reader observe this process. In the following passage, Michael does precisely this:

It could even be that, as a whole, Emily Brontë's *Wuthering Heights* constitutes a concerted investigation into 'learned' cruelty in the family; that is, how patterns of cruelty are internalized and reproduced by family members. This is particularly true as regards the 'family unit' of Hindley, Heathcliff, and Hareton, where sadistic behaviour is passed on from one member to the other. However, Jan Theiling would refute this view. For Theiling, in his book *Violence and the Victorian Novel* (London: Witz, 1991), cruelty in *Wuthering Heights* is 'predicated on randomness and has no meaning attached to it: it is beyond the author's control, and that is why it is so chilling' (p. 32). While Hareton's hanging of puppies from a chairback in chapter seventeen certainly falls into the category of random, meaningless cruelty, Theiling's thesis surely underplays the extent to which Brontë purposefully and coherently develops the theme of cruelty throughout her novel. Indeed, in *Brontë's Passion* (Leeds: Keiner, 1997), Nina Davies suggests that 'the study of premeditated, systematic cruelty is the author's main objective' (p. 87). While this perhaps goes too far now in the opposite direction, Davies at least recognizes Brontë's agency and guiding hand in the treatment of cruelty in *Wuthering Heights*. This, it seems to me, is crucial in understanding the novel, as I will now elaborate.

This is impressive writing: it is clear, finely balanced, and closely argued. Through exchanging views with other critics, taking what seems useful and rejecting that which does not, Michael's own position – that cruelty is treated purposefully by Brontë, and is not 'beyond [her] control' – crystallizes powerfully by the end of the 'sounding board' session.

The critic as 'springboard'

Finally, let's see how we can take an idea from a critic and use it as a springboard from which to leap off into our own discussion. Imagine you're a Film Studies student. You're reading Donna Haraway's intriguing book, *Simians, Cyborgs, and Women: The Reinvention of Nature* (New York: Routledge, 1991), and encounter her suggestive idea that 'cyborgs' are emancipated from patriarchal history since:

> The cyborg has no origin story in the Western sense [. . .]. The cyborg would not recognize the Garden of Eden; it is not made of mud and cannot dream of returning to dust.
>
> (pp. 150–1)

Then you start thinking about the renegade androids (cyborg 'replicants') in *Blade Runner*, the film version of Philip K. Dick's novel *Do Androids Dream of Electric Sheep?* At the beginning of the film, Nexus-6 androids – physically practically indistinguishable from humans – made by the Tyrell Corporation, have been banished from Earth to live on Mars. A small group, led by the alpha-android Roy Batty, escape and return to Earth with the intention of seeking out their 'creator', Dr Eldon Tyrell. Although Haraway's cyborg theory argues that cyborgs have no yearnings for origins, you suddenly realize that this journey could be interpreted precisely as an attempt to return to a point of origin – to the Garden of Eden (in this case the Garden of Eldon):

Whereas Haraway's cyborgs are empowered by not being shackled to patriarchal myths of origin, Dick's recalcitrant androids seem to be saying that this emancipation is not enough. Finally, the deep-seated desire to understand one's beginnings, and the feeling of having been betrayed by one's creator, drive them to return to Eden (Eldon) even though this leads to their violent deaths at the hands of the blade runners whose job it is to 'retire' – destroy – any replicants they find. For Dick, these desires and emotions are part of what it means to be alive, and actually define the quality of being human far more meaningfully than the Voigt-Kampff test employed by the blade runners to measure pupil fluctuation in subjects suspected of being replicants.

If you hadn't read Haraway, you might not have been nudged into this fruitful line of thought, and never have considered *Blade Runner* as a 'return to Eden' fantasy.

The counter-argument

Consider the case. You are halfway through a Media Studies essay on the history of British television, and are arguing that the so-called 'golden age' of TV in the mid to late 1970s is a fabrication created by nostalgic forty-somethings. Alongside the best of recent programming, such as 'The Royle Family' with Caroline Aherne and 'Ground Force' with Alan Titchmarsh, often-lauded 'golden-age' series like 'George and Mildred' and 'The Good Life' pale into insignificance, you insist. And then you remember truly great shows like 'Fawlty Towers', 'The Liver Birds', 'You and Me', 'Dr Who' (with Tom Baker), and 'The Professionals'. Not only that, but there are plenty of works of criticism in the library to tell you exactly *why* these were great programmes. Oh dear . . . Drawing attention to these series and books would scuttle your argument, or so you fear, and consequently you decide to ignore them altogether.

Now it might come as a surprise, but you'd be better off doing exactly the opposite and conceding the existence of alternative, perhaps equally tenable, views to your own: in other words, 'counter-arguments'. The counter-argument could be acknowledged in our Media Studies essay in the following manner:

> Although increased budgeting, rationalization, and an improved support system for new writers have led to a steady rise in the overall standard of programming on British television since the beginning of the nineties, it would be misleading to suggest that the so-called 'golden age' of television in this country in the late 1970s is a complete fabrication. As Edward Foreman points out in *The Best of British Television* (Liverpool: Quark, 1998), 'series such as "Fawlty Towers" and "The Good Life" set new standards of quality and sophistication for British comedy against which current writers and producers should still feel obliged to measure themselves' (p. 76). Yet while Foreman is undoubtedly right to emphasize the achievement of these earlier programmes, it is debatable whether they ought to remain an acid test for modern television, which has different concerns, and responds to different cultural and social conditions.

By allowing readers to see counter-arguments, you win their trust. Besides, you may find that your standpoint remains valid, or is even strengthened by comparison with others. Equally importantly, you show your tutor that you've done the legwork and researched your topic thoroughly. A one-sided argument impresses no one. From the reader's point of view it is much more exciting to see evidence for *and* against something. In fact, this is the only way anyone can judge how persuasive your argument really is.

Experienced writers routinely acknowledge 'weaknesses' in their argument because they know that, paradoxically, this helps to authorize their views. There's a good example of the way in which this works in a book by John Nicholson called *Men and Women: How Different Are They?* (Oxford: Oxford University Press, 1984):

> The aim of this book is to identify the most influential popular beliefs about 'typically' masculine and feminine behaviour, and

then see how well our intuitions stand up to objective testing. Most of the evidence I shall be considering has been obtained by researchers working in laboratories, using scientific methods. The fact that it has been gathered in this way does not give it any magical status. Nor are interpretations based on such evidence necessarily right, any more than our intuitions – that is, feelings that have not been exposed to the full rigours of scientific testing – are inevitably wrong. When the two are in conflict, my instinct as a scientist is to favour interpretations based on well-constructed experiments over those which are not, especially when the subject-matter is as emotionally involving and prejudice-ridden as human behaviour. But it is important to recognize the shortcomings as well as the advantages of so-called 'objective' evidence.

(pp. 1–2)

Hear, hear! This is a perfect example of how to win the trust and respect of your reader. Rather than assume arrogantly that scientific research is superior to intuition or popular belief in every case, Nicholson concedes that 'official' science is also flawed. A little further on he strengthens his 'unbiased' credentials by pointing out that 'the laboratory is an artificial environment, with its own rules and conventions, in which people may not behave in the same way as they do in normal life' (p. 2). All this helps draw the reader into a riveting discussion on how few 'real' differences there actually appear to be between women and men (or at least *appeared* to be in 1984, when the book was published).

I want to leave you with one last example of how giving the counter-argument helps win over the reader. In his pioneering study, *The Making of the English Working Class* (London: Victor Gollancz, 1968), E. P. Thompson argues for a revised history of the massacre by government troops of radicals and protesters at St Peter's Fields in Manchester, August 1819 (the so-called battle of 'Peterloo'). He asserts that the massacre was not a regrettable accident, but the result of a predetermined plan to disperse the meeting with force and thus send a bloody message to other potential dissidents. After stating his opinion, however,

Thompson does not balk at acknowledging some cogent opposing perspectives:

> This [Thompson's belief that Lord Liverpool's government had decided in advance to break up the meeting with troops] has to be said again, since it has been suggested recently [by Donald Read] that Peterloo was an affair, in part unpremeditated, in part arising from the exacerbated relations in Manchester itself, but in no sense any part of a considered policy of Government repression.
>
> (p. 749)

While obviously disagreeing, Thompson doesn't dismiss his antagonist's whole thesis out of hand. Instead he praises Read's book, *Peterloo* (Manchester: Manchester University Press, 1947), as a study which 'does much to place the event in its local context' (p. 749). Such manoeuvres – and they are manoeuvres (Read is damned with faint praise) – have the effect of putting Thompson in a better light. Because he has taken account of opposing views, readers are more likely to trust his interpretation of events. As soon as one senses that an author is trying to hide evidence, the Nixon-effect occurs, and we react vigorously against the argument being presented.

Note:

1 Work out how the **question** is structured before you decide how to organize your essay.
2 **Engage** with the critical debate, without being swamped by it.
3 **Acknowledge** counter-arguments.

Chapter 3

More on the middle section: linkage

Many students find it difficult to move smoothly between ideas in their essays, even though awkward transitions mean a bumpy ride for the reader. But when you are deep in thought, you might not even realize you *have* finished one point and started another, let alone have considered how best to do it. Worry not, gentle reader. In bite-sized chunks, this chapter explains the physical mechanics of linking sentences and paragraphs, ideas and sections. And not only is linkage easier than you might think; once you get the hang of it, you'll be amazed at how much more integrated and polished your essays suddenly appear.

Linking ideas & sentences

A man went into a shop. He wanted to speak to the manager about some faulty goods. The manager was not there.

Now this may make perfect sense, but it is annoyingly fitful to read. It is difficult to follow the sense of the passage across the full stops because the sentences are not linked. Compare the following revised version:

> A man went into a shop to speak to the manager about some faulty goods. However, the manager was not there.

This is much better. There is a greater degree of integration and logical momentum. Note that I've achieved this transformation without altering any of the ideas in the passage; I've merely made their logical relationship to each other more obvious, using link words such as 'to' and 'however'. One could go a step further:

> A man went into a shop to speak to the manager about some faulty goods, but the manager was not there.

This is perhaps best of all. However, be careful not to create monstrously long sentences. If you link too many things together, the result will be as incomprehensible as if you had not linked anything at all.

How does this translate into university or college writing? Compare the following two examples, and ask yourself which is more effective:

> Critic X argues that television has a limited impact on popular culture. Critic Y believes its influence is pervasive. Our ability to judge the issue may be severely compromised by our historical proximity to it. The real influence that television exerts on modern life may only become apparent with retrospect.

or:

> Critic X argues that television has a limited impact on popular culture. Critic Y, on the other hand, believes its influence is pervasive. But our ability to judge the issue may be severely compromised by our historical proximity to it. Indeed, the real

influence that television exerts on modern life may only become apparent with retrospect.

I hope you chose the latter (link elements underlined). I'll end this section with some helpful linking phrases:

Yet	In order to
But	Instead of
However	Having said that
Nevertheless	In contrast
Despite	On the contrary
Bearing that in mind	On the other hand
Beyond that	Perhaps
Because of this	Moreover
For instance	Furthermore
For example	As well as
While	As a matter of fact

Some to use with caution:

Clearly
Indeed
, then, . . . (as in, 'To conclude, then, I want to suggest that . . .')
In fact

And a few to avoid as you would people with peeling skin, wearing sunglasses, who moan 'Food! Food!' when they see you (not British holidaymakers on Majorca – zombies!):

Actually
Basically
Thus
Therefore

Linking paragraphs & sections

We've been studying linkage within and between sentences; now we are going to move up in scale to look at paragraphs and sections. In any essay, the larger or 'macro'-argument will almost certainly be comprised of a series of smaller sections, or 'micro'-arguments. These may well seem self-contained, each addressing discrete points or themes; but, in principle, all of them work towards establishing your wider proposition. I say 'in principle', because, for your mini-sections to add up to an ungainsayable whole, they have to be linked together properly. You see, weak-spots in essays frequently lie not in individual points, but in the gaps between points – not in the things you say, but in the things you *don't*. In short, if you omit to build bridges between sections in your essay, your argument will appear disjointed. The reader will struggle more and more to retain the sense of your argument, and eventually give up.

There are several good examples of transitions to be found in Scott McEathron's recent essay, 'Wordsworth, *Lyrical Ballads*, and the Problem of Peasant Poetry', which appeared in *Nineteenth-Century Literature* 54 (1999), 1–26. To put you in the picture, McEathron explores 'the relationship between Wordsworth's rustic poetry and the so-called "peasant" and "working-class" verse of the late eighteenth and early nineteenth centuries' (p. 1). The larger question posed is whether or not Wordsworth is justified in his claim to be the sole poet of 'low and rustic life' (as the mighty-browed bard puts it in his Preface to *Lyrical Ballads*).

In the sections of the essay I want to home in on, McEathron scrutinizes the work of earlier, arguably more 'genuine' rustic poets. First up is the much-maligned eighteenth-century 'thresher-poet', Stephen Duck. In this particular micro-argument, McEathron describes how many literary reviewers of the day refused to take 'low-born' poets like Duck seriously, associating them with ignorance, dirty hands, and farm animals(!!).

Now, in the micro-argument that immediately follows, McEathron reveals that not *all* literary critiques of peasant poetry boiled down to snide comments about the supposed poor hygiene and indifferent education of peasant poets. For example, Henry Mackenzie wrote a favourable and very influential review of his countryman, Scots dialect poet Robert Burns (1759–1796), in which the matter of Burns's low birth was explicitly described as irrelevant to his poetical merit. But – and this is my point – McEathron doesn't simply switch from utter darkness (critics dismissed peasant poets), to bright light (critics no longer did this). He installs a dimmer switch and turns the light up gradually:

> Overlapping with these satirical dismissals of peasant poetry, however, and gathering steam late in the century, was a strain of serious-minded, conscientious criticism that recognized that the habitual critical default to a peasant-poet stereotype threatened the credibility of poet and reviewer alike.
>
> (p. 8)

This is very skilful writing. The passage quite literally 'overlaps' the old and new points, moving into the new section (about 'serious-minded, conscientious criticism') via a recapitulation of the old one (about 'satirical dismissals of peasant poetry' by prejudiced critics). You'll see what I mean more clearly, perhaps, if I present McEathron's discussion as a schematic (see p. 30). Without a 'transition', the move between micro-arguments would be like shifting gear without first depressing the clutch.

Transitions needn't be elaborate affairs. Here is an example from an English essay on Wordsworth's and Coleridge's famous 1798 collection of verse, *Lyrical Ballads*. After a short section on the poem, 'Lines Written a Few Miles Above Tintern Abbey', we discover that:

> Wordsworth develops his ideas about time further in this poem and imagines the influence that the past will have on the future.

Immediately afterwards, attention shifts to a second piece from the collection, 'The Ruined Cottage'. The respective micro-arguments are linked by a simple remark about shared chronology:

Micro-argument 1
Culturally snobbish
reviewers played on popular
stereotypes of peasant poets
to dismiss their writing. E.g.
attacks on Duck.

Transition section
While many reviewers
continued to dismiss low-born
writers, the situation began to
change . . .

Micro-argument 2
Reviewers began to review
in a more responsible
fashion; the circumstances
of an author's birth, while
impossible to forget
entirely, were increasingly
seen as impediments to
assessing the poetry
itself. E.g. Mackenzie's
review of Burns.

Written at the same time as 'Tintern Abbey', 'The Ruined Cottage' shows clearly that Man and Nature are interwoven.

Now, as you can perhaps gauge even from these short extracts, neither section of the essay has very much to do with the other. One looks at the connection between past and future; the other at the interaction of man and nature. Indeed, in terms of logical progression, the essay's entire argument scores a resounding *nul points*. Nevertheless, we *are* given fair warning whenever the argument is about to shift in focus, which conjures at least an impression of this student's agency and control. (For the cynics among you, I'm not suggesting for a moment that this is any substitute for a carefully thought-out argument.)

'Signposts'

It is very important to reassure your reader that you are in control of your argument. It is *your* discussion, so don't leave people to wander around in it like lost things. Rather, lead them through each section purposefully, letting them know exactly what is happening as you do it. I want to look now at an essay called 'Art and Audience' by Nick Zangwill, published in *Journal of Aesthetics and Art Criticism* 57 (1999), 315–32. It's a racy piece, controversial even, that asks whether a work of art necessarily has or even needs a relationship with an audience (Zangwill adopts the provocative position that it does not). The informal tone of this essay might be a touch *too* intimate for some, and I would certainly be wary myself of including quite so many personal interjections. But the important thing to note is how hard Zangwill works to avoid losing his reader. In fact, there is little opportunity to get lost in Zangwill's argument. This is because, although it twists and turns like a twisty-turny thing in a particularly twisty (not to mention turny) mood, it has been scrupulously well signposted.

What do I mean by a 'signpost'? On the first page of Zangwill's article we find a good example:

> I shall come back to some of these distinctions. [. . .] But we might as well note straightaway that . . .

As you can see, signposts are phrases or short passages that tell the reader what is happening, or about to happen, in terms of argument or in the way an essay is organized. As to *why* we signpost essays . . . Perhaps it would help if I asked you to visualize Zangwill's argument on the relationship between art and audience as a tangled forest. Go on – humour me.

There are many paths weaving through this forest; some of them intersect, some are dead-ends, and some lead into dangerous quagmires. Undaunted, Zangwill heads off into the forest. As he walks through the undergrowth, he stops to examine interesting-looking flowers, ferns, or mushrooms; he pauses to compare fauna from different parts of the wooded area; he also studies the wildlife. Naturally, he wants to share what he has discovered with other people, and to this end prepares a trail for them to follow. Because the forest is tangled and the path winding, he erects signposts at potentially confusing places. These will guide and reassure fellow walkers, as well as giving them useful tips about the things they are going to see. Take another look at Zangwill's first signpost:

> I shall come back to some of these distinctions. [. . .] But we might as well note straightaway that . . .

This tells walkers (1) that they are about to change paths, even though they haven't finished looking at all the interesting things on the present route yet; and (2) not to worry, because there'll be an opportunity to return in a while. All along the trail, Zangwill puts himself into his reader's shoes; he knows exactly at what stage in his discussion they will need help and encouragement. He *never* leaves them to find their own way from one part of his argument to another.

It is never too late to add signposts. In fact, it only really becomes clear where they need to be erected once your essay is in the final proof-reading stages and you gain a clearer overview of how your argument reads.

Experienced writers routinely help their readers out as their discussion develops or becomes more complex. Take the following extract from Thomas McFarland's essay, 'Coleridge: Prescience, Tenacity and the Origin of Sociality', *Romanticism* 4.1 (1998), 40–59:

> Whatever Coleridge was, a chameleon he was not. Indeed, it might even be said that the whole point of this paper is to demonstrate how baseless is such a charge. No one has ever been more constant in his opinions or more tenacious in his

intellectual attitudes and viewpoints than was Coleridge. But he has in recent years been enveloped in a miasma of misconception, and grossly, even ludicrously mistaken views have sometimes prevailed.

To dispel, or begin to dispel, that miasma of misconception, therefore, an extended concluding example must be joined to the three already summoned. It will serve to illustrate still a fourth aspect of Coleridge's all-pervading intellectual tenacity.

(p. 51)

I like this passage: it's gutsy, bad-tempered, and shoots from the hip. A 'miasma of misconception' – what a great way of saying that other Coleridge critics have got things completely wrong! Ditto 'ludicrously mistaken views'. But the primary purpose of the passage is to inform the reader that they will shortly be studying a fourth example of Coleridge's intellectual tenacity:

> . . . an extended concluding example must be joined to the three already summoned.

In other words, the passage, for all its attitude and 'presence', is essentially a signpost, albeit a very entertaining one.

Changing direction

As long as you explain *when* and *why* you are doing something new, you can perform a series of 180-degree turns while doing cartwheels and whistling 'God Save the Queen', and still keep your reader with you. Conversely, if you change direction without saying anything at all, the sudden centrifugal forces could send your readers spinning off into the undergrowth, where wild animals will come and eat them up.

The following example is taken from an essay on Marcel Duchamp's attitude to the 'machine age', written by an Art History student called Anna:

> Until now we have discussed Duchamp's attitude to the machine age specifically in terms of the scientific aspect of the age. We will now discuss the influences of philosophical thought and literature of the time.

Apart from the fact that the sentence would benefit from having 'the scientific aspect of the age' shortened to 'scientific aspects', it is a well-written transition that clearly announces the author's intention to head off in a new direction.

While you certainly should not insert clarificatory sections after every other paragraph – this would be torturous to read – it is in your own interest to give your reader a little help at seminal junctures in your argument. Anyone can write an essay that quickly loses its readers (French literary theorists do this all the time); but it takes real skill to keep your reader with you all the way through.

We'll look at one more example of clear signposting before imminent changes of tack. It is taken from an essay that explores whether or not nineteenth-century writing typically represents women as belonging to a domestic sphere. Jane, an English student, has just argued that Margaret Hale, the heroine of Elizabeth Gaskell's novel, *North and South* (1855), is repeatedly associated with domesticity. Now Jane prepares to start a new section in which she will inaugurate a discussion of the novel's *male* characters:

> Just as Margaret represents the feminine, domestic sphere, the novel's male protagonists of both classes – Thornton, the mill-owner and Nicholas Higgins, the high-minded trade unionist – are shown to represent the 'masculine realm of competitiveness and aggression'.

Leaving aside the rather uncritical gender clichés that are flying around like . . . well, flying things, and the weak (because couched in the passive) 'are shown to', we find a plain but effective linking phrase – 'Just as' – that neatly connects the new section to the old.

Prêt à porter

I'll end this chapter with a collection of 'ready-to-wear' linking sentences and phrases. Perhaps you'll find one that fits or can be adapted to your particular needs.

Changing direction

(a) If my discussion up to this point has emphasized X, we should also devote some time to considering Y.

(b) While this was true regarding foreign policy under X, the situation changed significantly under Y, as I will now outline.

(c) At this stage in our argument, it is appropriate to voice the following question: how far can one . . .

(d) At the beginning of this essay, I contended X, Y, and Z; before we proceed any further, it should be noted that/I wish to clarify that . . .

(e) [Following a discussion of High Street spending in the 1990s] If, as I suggested in my earlier overview, shop-keepers had reason enough to be disgruntled in the winter of 1993, the second half of the decade saw levels of spending unrivalled since the mid-1980s. I want to look more closely now at the period 1994–1999.

Linking a point to critical opinion

(f) My contention that Keats deliberately resists displacing thoughts of illness – which must have been very present in 1819 – onto his poetry receives some important, if not unequivocal support from Ima C. Ritic's recent book, *Only the Sick Die Young: Keats and Medical Imagery* (London: Nosuchpress, 2000). Ritic suggests that . . .

(g) As we have seen, David Evans offers a persuasive overview of King Francis's court but one that fails, it seems to me, to take into account the full extent to which preferment of family members influenced court appointments during the monarch's reign. That the practice was rife, far more so than Evans allows, can be established from a glance at the web of familial relationships connecting office holders between 1746 and 1773. For instance, out of seven Royal Chancellors in this period, five were directly related to the King. Out of nine Court Jesters . . .

Linking two poems

(h) [Following a discussion of Keats's 'Specimen of an Induction to a Poem', written spring 1816] If this poem represents an early critique of neoclassical diction, it is a critique that took powerful form some six months later. In Keats's sonnet 'On First Looking into Chapman's Homer' (October 1816), we see how . . .

Linking two events

(i) While the Cato Street Conspiracy to blow up parliament in February 1820 proved a disaster (particularly for the would-be perpetrators) of almost farcical proportions, the massacre of protesters at St Peter's Fields in Manchester six months earlier was nothing less than tragic. The event, which came to be known as the Battle of Peterloo, with ironic echoes of Waterloo, marked a watershed in the struggle between government and radical opposition.

Note:

1 **Link** sentences, paragraphs, and sections.
2 **Signpost** your argument clearly.
3 Whenever you change direction, **warn** your reader in advance. Assume they get lost easily, rather than hoping they will be able to follow your argument like Indian scouts across the plains and over the hills.

Chapter 4

How to write conclusions

If introductions are all about making a first impression, conclusions are about leaving a last impression, which is equally important. Apart from your bibliography, the conclusion is the last thing your tutor will read before he or she enters a mark in the ledger of life. Again, as with all stages of the essay, there are things to do and things to avoid, and the purpose of this chapter is to tell you exactly what these are.

In the following sections, I'm going to talk about *summary* and *discursive* conclusions. The first is retrospective in character, and gathers together the thoughts developed in the course of your essay. It is useful when you are trying to prove a case or clinch a larger point. The 'discursive' conclusion, by contrast, continues developing your argument until the last full stop. It tends to work well with assignments that are wide-ranging in scope and perhaps more conversational in tone than 'point-proving' essays. Let us consider both types of conclusion now in more detail.

'SUMMARY' CONCLUSIONS

Weighing up your own argument

If you are writing an essay that sets out to establish something fairly concrete, it is a good idea to use your final paragraph to weigh up the main arguments rehearsed in your discussion. This way the reader gets a quick 'refresher' on what the essay was about, and you get an opportunity to draw your salient points into clear focus one last time. I'll begin by looking at a summary conclusion from an English student named Katy. Her essay explores different critical approaches to the work of Romantic poet, John Keats (1795–1821). The first (the 'traditional' view) argues that Keats's poetry arises out of a desire to transcend or disengage from contemporary politics and 'real life'; the second (the 'materialist' approach) asserts that, on the contrary, Keats engages rigorously with the events of his day in his poetry. Katy's final paragraph reads as follows:

> As I have shown, both schools of criticism under consideration provide inadequate accounts of Keats's poetry. Traditional approaches fail to consider the influence of society and politics upon the imagination (that is, the unconscious 'place' Keats inhabited during his composition), while materialist criticism does not take into account the possibility that Keats was indirectly (subconsciously) affected by what he saw around him, rather than directly and consciously. However, as I have demonstrated in my essay, the respective opposing stances adopted by these critiques can be resolved into a view of Keats that both recognizes the influence of specific, historical conditions on his compositional process and, at the same time, acknowledges the role of the transcendent and transcending poetic imagination.

This is a pleasure to read. Katy resists plumping for one or the other approach as a panacean, 'cure-all' solution to the problems of reading Keats; instead she identifies blinkered perspectives in both schools of criticism. Her conclusion broadly reiterates what her larger discussion has illustrated in detail, namely that: (1) traditional views of Keats as an isolated genius, immured or oblivious to the realities of day-to-day life, fail to recognize the influence political events had on his writing; (2) more recent historicist or materialist accounts, which argue that all literature should be understood in terms of specific historical contexts, do not always appreciate that the influence of turbulent political times on Keats was often indirect and nebulous, rather than immediate and obvious. After scrutinizing the merits and de-merits of each school of criticism, Katy concludes that a compromise between the two approaches offers a more integrated reading of Keats.

The style, too, is impressive. Take another look at the last sentence:

> However, as I have demonstrated in my essay, the respective opposing stances adopted by these critiques can be resolved into a view of Keats that both recognizes . . . and, at the same time, acknowledges . . .

I like the phrase 'resolved into'. It's just another way of saying 'can be combined', but it's more interesting and betokens a developed critical vocabulary.

Improvements? I would delete the word 'subconsciously' in parentheses halfway through the paragraph because it adds very little, and perhaps even confuses matters:

> . . . while materialist criticism does not take into account the possibility that Keats was indirectly ~~(subconsciously)~~ affected by what he saw around him, rather than directly and consciously.

I'm uneasy, too, about the first set of parentheses:

> Traditional approaches fail to consider the influence of society and politics upon the imagination (that is, the unconscious 'place' Keats inhabited during his composition).

This seems to suggest that Keats's poetic imagination *was* 'unconscious' after all, thus reinforcing the traditional view of Keats as a transcendent, ethereal genius, the conduit of the muses, who wrote great poetry without really knowing how.

I would also tinker with the last sentence:

> However, as I have demonstrated in my essay, the respective opposing stances adopted by these critiques can be resolved into a view of Keats that both recognizes the influence of specific, historical conditions on his compositional process and, at the same time, acknowledges the role of the transcendent and transcending poetic imagination.

This is a bit cumbersome; a more wieldy version would be:

> However, as I have demonstrated in my essay, these opposing critiques can be resolved into a view of Keats that both recognizes the influence of history on his writing and, at the same time, acknowledges the role of the transcendent and transcending poetic imagination.

Under the microscope

How does Katy manage to summarize her argument so clearly and concisely? Let's look at the passage again from a technical perspective. Here is the revised second sentence:

> (2) Traditional approaches fail to consider the influence of society and politics upon the imagination, while materialist criticism does not take into account the possibility that Keats was indirectly affected by what he saw around him, rather than directly and consciously.

If we boiled it down to its components, we'd end up with:

> Traditional approaches fail to do A; while materialist approaches fail to do B.

40

Or, reduced even further:

X fails to do A; while Y fails to do B.

This is an example of what we might call a 'seesaw' sentence. The cadencies of grammar and logic rise to 'while', before falling again. Indeed, the structural logic of the sentence pivots on this word. As soon as we reach it we know that the second half of the sentence must contain a point of contrast. Consider the following formula by way of comparison:

X fails to do A; while Y fails to do A.

Clearly, this does not work. It doesn't make sense because it doesn't *concatenate*; that is, the individual elements in the series do not follow on logically or conform to our expectations. The last sentence in Katy's conclusion is a good illustration of how strong concatenation helps the reader retain the sense of even lengthy passages:

> However, as I have demonstrated in my essay, these opposing critiques can be resolved into a view of Keats that both recognizes the influence of history on his writing and, at the same time, acknowledges the role of the transcendent and transcending poetic imagination.

This can be represented as:

> X can be resolved into a view that both recognizes A and, at the same time, registers B.

The moment we read:

. . . that both recognizes A

we are waiting for something along the lines of:

and, at the same time, does B.

There is a reassuring sense of inevitability about this essay's sentence structure, because Katy weaves strands of logic into the very fabric of her writing. You can be sure that her essay was not dashed off and handed in on the way to the student bar. She read over her work, made changes, tried things out, and then handed it in. And *then* went to the bar.

Common pitfalls

Let's look at another 'summary' conclusion, this time not quite so accomplished, from a student called Mike. The question was:

> 'For all the over-sized projections of masculinity masquerading in Mary Shelley's *Frankenstein*, the novel's male protagonists are virtual case-studies in neurosis, hysteria, uncertainty, and angst.' Discuss.

This was his final paragraph:

> *Frankenstein* shows many uncertainties in the identities of the male characters as to their positions in an uncertain and changing world, where the relationship between Man and God was, through science, being constantly questioned. Through modern readings of the text the characters of Victor Frankenstein and his creation have merged and blurred as if their characters have in fact become one. The novel can therefore be said to contain its neurosis, hysteria, uncertainty, and angst in its examination of humanity, creation, and nature. Placing these uncertainties into the context of contemporary society.

To be frank, Mike, it's a bit of a mess. Whereas Katy's sentences concatenate, these do not – even though they are much shorter. We'll have to work hard to improve things.

Although one could be forgiven for not realizing it, there are two main points being made in this paragraph: (1) rapid changes in society, especially in the area of science, aroused anxieties in early nineteenth-century society; (2) Mary Shelley explores these anxieties, particularly as they affect the male characters in her novel. In order to make these points audible, we need to reduce the background noise. Here is the first sentence again:

> (1) *Frankenstein* shows many <u>uncertainties</u> in <u>the</u> identities of <u>the</u> male characters as to their positions in an <u>uncertain</u> and changing world, where the relationship between Man and God was, through science, being constantly questioned.

The Force definitely wasn't with Mike when he wrote this. To start with, the underlined bits are clumsy and repetitious. Secondly, is 'shows' at the beginning of the sentence the right word? 'Explores' or 'considers' would be more appropriate, to my mind. And can we really say that the novel shows uncertainties *in* the identities of the male characters? Surely the male characters in the novel experience uncertainties *about* identity, which is slightly different. Finally, although inexperienced writers often resort to the phrase 'as to', used in the sense of 'concerning' or 'regarding', it seldom works satisfactorily. It is usually better to write 'concerning' or 'regarding'.

Sentence (1) needs to be rearranged along these lines:

> Mary Shelley's novel considers the problem of male identity in a changing world, where rapid advances in science meant that even the relationship between Man and God was being questioned.

This is a lot better now. Moving on to the second sentence – Mike notes that 'Frankenstein' is often, but incorrectly, assumed to be the name of the 8-foot-tall 'monster', rather than the scientist who created him:

> (2) Through modern readings of the text the characters of Victor Frankenstein and his creation have merged and become blurred as if their characters have in fact become one.

This comment is in the wrong place, since it has no logical connection with either sentence (1) or (3). It is also conspicuous because it introduces new information (more on this later). To make matters worse, due to poor expression the interpolated material is spectacularly inaccurate. Confusion over the creature's and creator's name has not occurred 'through modern readings of the text'. Quite the opposite – confusion has arisen through people *not* reading the text. No one who has read Mary Shelley's novel would confuse Victor Frankenstein with the 'monster'. Mike knows this, of course, but has not found a way to say it unambiguously.

To cap it all, the sentence is repetitious:

> . . . the characters of Victor Frankenstein and his creation have merged and blurred as if their characters have in fact become one.

If two things have merged and blurred, we do not need to add that they have become one. Doh! We would be well advised to jettison the second sentence altogether.

We'd better proceed to the third sentence:

> (3) The novel can therefore be said to contain its neurosis, hysteria, uncertainty, and angst in its examination of humanity, creation, and nature.

It's the same story here, I'm afraid – sloppy expression. Can we really say the novel *contains* 'neurosis, hysteria, uncertainty, and angst'? Isn't it rather the case that the novel *explores* its *characters'* neuroses? Again, there is a subtle but significant difference between what Mike means and what he has actually written. The sentence should be amended to:

> The novel therefore explores neurosis, hysteria, uncertainty, and angst in its examination of humanity, creation, and nature.

The most unfortunate moment in this conclusion has been saved right until the end:

(4) Placing these uncertainties into the context of contemporary society.

Whoops! Fancy ending on an incomplete sentence. What an ignominious exit! The verb needs immediate surgery if this passage is going to make sense to anyone other than Mike:

> Mary Shelley places all these uncertainties within the context of contemporary nineteenth-century society.

Let's reassemble the conclusion, bearing in mind all we have discussed so far:

> Mary Shelley's novel considers the problem of male identity in a changing world, where rapid advances in science meant that even the relationship between Man and God was being questioned. The novel therefore explores neurosis, hysteria, uncertainty, and angst in its examination of humanity, creation, and nature. Mary Shelley places all these uncertainties within the context of contemporary nineteenth-century society.

OK, I think we have done all we can with the material at hand. At least it's grammatical now. But in terms of argument, this conclusion couldn't punch its way out of a wet paper bag, as I'll explain.

Internal coherency again

Even in the improved version of the final paragraph, the first two sentences do not stand in a particularly meaningful relationship to each other. This is despite the slightly desperate (and thoroughly bogus) 'therefore', which wouldn't fool any tutor worth his or her salt.

Let me elucidate. The first sentence says that *Frankenstein* considers how males relate to 'an uncertain and changing world', where science is questioning 'the relationship between Man and God'. The second shifts focus to suggest that the novel 'therefore' explores 'neuroses, hysteria, uncertainty, and angst' through examining 'humanity, creation, and nature'. There just isn't any logical progression here that I can discern. We have not arrived at the second sentence because of some point that has been clinched magnificently and irrefutably in the first. What is *actually* happening is that both sentences are telling us something slightly different about the novel.

Although Mike's final paragraph is, on first glance at least, a 'summary' conclusion, it doesn't really summarize an argumentative process. Mike was probably a little unsure himself about what his essay had demonstrated, and this shows in his conclusion. Consequently, the reader is left in some doubt as to what Mike's final position actually is. Which brings me on to my next theme . . .

Making your point clear

Your tutor must feel satisfied that some point has been established in your essay, and the best way of ensuring that this happens is to spell out exactly *what*. Louise, who answered the same question as Mike, does this quite effectively:

> During the course of this essay, I have argued that the novel *Frankenstein*, despite appearing to privilege the male voice, is a vehicle to undermine the oppressive masculine ideologies that seek to define, and indeed silence women.

Clear and purposeful sentences like this represent the difference between a low 2,ii and a high 2,i grade. If your essay has been tightly argued, you should be able to give a similarly succinct summary of your essay, too.

If I seem a little crotchety, it is only because the majority of Mike's mistakes have arisen purely because he has not read over his essay, checking that his words say exactly what he intends them to. He has presumed that I'll do the slog of working out what he means. Believe me, if you submit an assignment without casting a cold eye over it first, in the hope that your tutor will recognize the genius beneath the muddle, you're in for a rude awakening.

Answering the question

Another deficiency in Mike's conclusion lies in its failure to connect with the terms of the question. This, you'll remember, asked us to consider the proposition that even the most apparently confident male characters in *Frankenstein* are neurotic and angst-ridden:

> 'For all the over-sized projections of masculinity masquerading in Mary Shelley's *Frankenstein*, the novel's male protagonists are virtual case-studies in neurosis, hysteria, uncertainty, and angst.' Discuss.

Although Mike mentions key words such as 'neurosis' and 'uncertainty', his conclusion does not really address the critical scope of the question. Don't forget, he has been asked to think about over-sized projections of masculinity, so his conclusion should at least make passing reference to something that could cover for an over-sized projection of masculinity on a dark night. I am not suggesting that one repeat the question verbatim in the final paragraph. There is nothing worse than ending: 'and that is why I agree that male characters in *Frankenstein* are "virtual case-studies in neurosis, hysteria, uncertainty, and angst"'. However, one must at least pay lip-service to the question.

I have tried to do this in the following passage, which concludes an essay on 'Mary Shelley, Science, and Gender Politics':

> Against a backdrop of feminist polemic, Mary Shelley seeks to associate scientific advance with stereotypical masculinity, as embodied by the ambitious Victor Frankenstein and his gigantic creature. Conversely, the victims of science are all homely women such as Elizabeth and Justine, or else 'feminine' men like Clerval and the 'girlish' William. Each of these characters is murdered by the creature, who is the very emblem of scientific advance. Yet in spite of this directed and schematic treatment, one is tempted to ask how successful Shelley actually is in conflating social critique and feminist discourse. As I have argued in this essay, patriarchy's representatives – Victor, Walton, and the creature – are angst-ridden and neurotic, and

47

hardly role models of masculinity. Ultimately Shelley's novel reveals that, far from being masters of their own destiny, even the ostensible protagonists of change are subject to the wider doubts and uncertainties of the age. In a sense, Shelley's theory of masculine identity is refuted by her male characters themselves. Perhaps the message we should derive from *Frankenstein* is that the experience of technological advance cuts across – and still cuts across – gender boundaries, proving equally unsettling for both men and women.

The paragraph took a few attempts to get right, and would certainly benefit from some more tinkering; but I'm quite pleased with it. It summarizes my larger argument, restating the best points fairly lucidly. The reader gets my argument in 'headlines' – namely, that Shelley (1) genders society as 'feminine' and scientific advance as 'masculine'; (2) that she seeks to show how the pursuit of science is personally destructive as well as socially incohesive; (3) that such schematic gender politics tends to simplify the lived experience of social upheaval in the early nineteenth century.

Stylistically, the passage is fairly secure. I especially like the phrase 'against a backdrop of feminist polemic' (although I toyed with an alternative, 'from a palpably feminist perspective'). The paragraph is also tightly argued and internally coherent, as we can gauge by breaking it down into its components:

1 Mary Shelley presents scientific study and the ambition driving it as 'masculine',
→ 2 whereas the *victims* of science are all 'feminine'.
→ 3 Is Shelley successful in imposing a feminist narrative onto a social critique?
→ 4 Possibly not – Shelley's schematic (science = masculine/ predatory/bad, society = feminine/vulnerable/good) breaks down as the ostensibly super-'masculine' Victor and his creature turn out to be insecure, lonely, and afraid.
→ 5 The novel thus offers a different message to that Shelley intends: namely, that scientific advance is equally un- settling for both men and women.

If we reversed the order of any of these points, the paragraph would no longer make sense – the sure sign of a close argument.

Adding new material to the conclusion

Earlier, I complained that Mike had interpolated hitherto unseen material in his conclusion. Whether or not you should include new points in a 'summary' conclusion depends to some extent on what it is you want to add, and how you intend to add it. Avoid anything that opens up or requires further discussion. For instance, if I added the following sentence to my own *Frankenstein* conclusion, I would be doing myself a grave disservice:

> Mary Shelley's husband, Percy, revised the text of *Frankenstein* substantially and is responsible for much of the novel's overblown Latinate rhetoric. In one sense, we could say that Percy Shelley is himself an outsized masculine presence in Mary's novel.

No matter how intrinsically interesting this new point may be, it has no place in my conclusion because it is too close to the subject of my essay for comfort. The fact that Mary Shelley's husband helped edit her book could have considerable bearing on my larger argument, and should have been considered as a discrete point elsewhere. On the other hand, a more 'neutral' piece of new information, one with only a tangential relationship to my main themes, could be quite an effective way of drawing things to a close:

> As the modern world still struggles to come to terms with the technological revolution, and hitherto stable values are constantly renegotiated, Mary Shelley's novel of science and attendant responsibility retains all the relevance and poignancy it possessed in 1818.

'DISCURSIVE' CONCLUSIONS

The discursive conclusion offers a great deal of scope for flair and inventiveness. With this kind of ending, there is no need to worry inordinately about providing your reader with a final overview, or assiduously mapping a retrospective route through your arguments. Just continue developing your views until you drop!

Striking a tone

I'm going to look at a very energetic discursive conclusion, written by an English student called Stuart. His essay explores the cultural impact of postmodernism (don't worry about the technical terms – I'm more interested in how the conclusion is organized). I have included the last three paragraphs this time, which is where the final section of Stuart's essay begins:

> And what of the future? Well, since this essay has so far been broad and sweeping, it seems only fitting to sweep broadly across the future and try to foresee the fate of writing.

> Computers, and technology in general, have made information more accessible than ever before. There is no longer any absolute need for reference material to be physically present in libraries, as a large proportion of it can be stored digitally on silicon. Eventually, most books will be transcribed onto computers, and the need to buy them will diminish; all that will remain will be sentimental collectors' items. Ultimately, writers will be renamed 'typers' (or something which George Orwell would have been equally proud of), and literature will be produced solely in computer-readable format.

> This may be a distressing outlook for some, but it serves to amplify the illustration of the breaks that occur at the end of one form of art, and at the start of the next. I see a move to full computerization as dire, but this is only because I am used to my books, and relaxed into the present way that life operates.

There are, and always will be, people who do not want to 'make it new'. It is the responsibility of the strong and innovative artist to refute claims of stability and comfort, and to forge ahead, undaunted, and to create afresh.

This is all enthusiasm and verve. I love the conversational tone the passage strikes, and I really admire how Stuart communicates his thoughts to the reader so directly and effectively. The paragraph is not only easy to read – it's fun to read. Unlike with a 'summary' conclusion, there is no attempt to pull together all the points made so far in the essay. Indeed, apart from the reference to 'making it new', which pops up at various points in Stuart's discussion, the argument about writing practices of the future is run here for the first time.

Let's not order the ticker-tape parade just yet though – there are a couple of awkward moments. The first sentence in the third paragraph is a touch unclear because it is convoluted and poorly expressed:

> . . . but it serves to amplify the illustration of the breaks that occur at the end of one form of art, and at the start of the next.

Que? I'm also more than marginally inclined to worry about:

> I am used to my books, and relaxed into the present way that life operates.

'To relax into something'? I've never heard this expression before. I think the prose itself is rather too relaxed at this point! But these are minor gripes. In general, the conclusion is impressive.

The flourish

The flourish, which is an optional element in a conclusion, is a final bold statement to let your reader know that the essay has ended, and ended in style. While it can be effective in both summary and discursive conclusions, it lends itself particularly well to the latter. Stuart's essay affords a good example:

> It is the responsibility of the strong and innovative artist to refute claims of stability and comfort, and to forge ahead, undaunted, and to create afresh.

Ah! Walter Pater is alive and well and living in Aberystwyth. OK, if we were being curmudgeonly we might ask (putting on our grammar caps and muttering darkly about missing genitive subjects), '*whose* "claims of stability and comfort"?' But this flourish is a stylish end to a thoughtful and thought-provoking conclusion that, despite the odd uneven patch, any tutor would enjoy reading.

Note:

1. Decide whether your essay needs a **discursive** or **summary** conclusion.
2. Ensure that your conclusion is **internally coherent**.
3. Check that it has **sufficient connection** with the terms and scope of the question.
4. Make sure that you establish, and are seen to establish, a **point** or **position**.

Chapter 5

Grammar & punctuation

No matter how impressive your ideas are, or how pretty your essay looks when it arrives in the print tray, bad grammar and poor spelling will instantly prejudice your tutor against you – and with good reason. The days of splurging your ideas out onto the page and letting the reader work out what you mean, are over. If all that mattered was the quality of your ideas, assessment could be done with you in the pub over a beer. But, in addition to having good ideas, you need to be able to show that you can communicate them precisely and economically (one of the so-called 'transferable' skills you will take with you when you leave university or college).

In 1818, the political radical and social reformer William Cobbett wrote a *Grammar of the English Language* with the aim of teaching an ill-educated, oppressed working class how to express themselves effectively. Bad grammar, as Cobbett realized, introduces ambiguity into a discussion. At best this detracts from the force of an argument; at worst it allows words to be twisted so that you appear to be saying something quite other than you intend. If you're not careful, a sentence can slip its leash and run rings around your efforts to impose some kind of meaning on it.

In this chapter, I focus on how to express yourself accurately and grammatically. I look at typical student errors, such as misuse of ''s', wrongly placed commas, commonly misspelled words, overuse of the passive, confusion over 'who' and 'whom', and poor hyphenation.

It's illogical, Jim!

It simply is not sufficient to tell yourself 'this reads a bit oddly, but my tutor will know what I mean'. Make sure your sentences *say exactly what you mean*, and *mean exactly what you say*. Many instances of clumsy grammar can be cleared up in this way. For a case in point, take a look at the following rather peculiar sentence:

> Of course, attitudes towards colonialism in the seventeenth century were much different from that of a twentieth-century reader.

One might be uneasy about the unsupported generalizations concerning attitudes towards colonialism; but, to stick with grammar for the moment, why is this sentence so odd? To start with, the plural noun 'attitudes' in the first half of the sentence needs to be balanced by the plural determiner 'those' in the second (not by the singular 'that'):

> Of course, attitude<u>s</u> towards colonialism in the seventeenth century were much different from <u>those</u> of a twentieth-century reader.

This makes a *little* more sense now. But the next problem is that the two halves of the sentence do not fit together very convincingly. Either we match A–A:

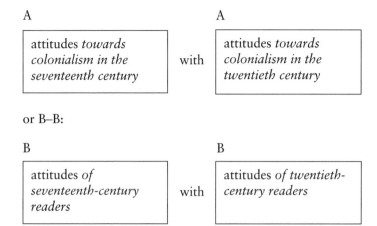

A   A

| attitudes *towards colonialism in the seventeenth century* | with | attitudes *towards colonialism in the twentieth century* |

or B–B:

B   B

| attitudes *of seventeenth-century readers* | with | attitudes *of twentieth-century readers* |

As things stand, we have a mixture of A–B, which is, not to beat around the bush, wrong. I'd be inclined to run with the first option:

> Of course, attitudes towards colonialism in the seventeenth century were much different from those in the twentieth century.

This is definitely an improvement, but the sentence is still slightly ambiguous. Are we talking about seventeenth-century colonialism, or seventeenth-century *attitudes* towards colonialism? On reflection, I think we should reformulate the sentence completely:

> Of course, seventeenth-century attitudes towards colonialism were very different from those in the twentieth century.

Now *that's* more like it. There was never anything wrong with the ideas in this sentence, particularly, just with the way they were communicated. You might say that grammar got in the way! Nevertheless, by working through alternatives – as you should always be prepared to do – we arrived at an elegant solution. Don't be satisfied with a sentence that seems even slightly strange. If it sounds funny or odd, then write it in a different way.

Here's another grammatical oddity. Can you spot what's wrong?

> According to Harrison and Wood they suggest there were two responses to XYZ.

We have a double subject – 'Harrison and Wood' and 'they'. Moreover, 'they suggest' is a virtual repetition of 'according to Harrison and Wood'. The sentence should either read:

> According to Harrison and Wood, there were two responses to XYZ.

or:

> Harrison and Wood suggest that there were two responses to XYZ.

Crazy commas

Other obstacles to writing clear, logical, and grammatical prose are presented by poor or sloppy punctuation, in particular wrongly used commas:

> The most striking thing about *Dr Faustus* is its humanity, its compassion.

I quite like the sentiments of this statement, but grammatically it is deeply suspect. The comma trips the reader up because it does not fulfil its proper role (that of separating items in a list or providing a mental breathing space). Instead it has been used incorrectly as a conjunction – that is, as a joining word like 'and', 'or', 'but'. This student clearly means:

> The most striking thing about *Dr Faustus* is its humanity <u>and</u> compassion.

Problems arise due to sloppy grammar; the specific error here is *parataxis* (the technical term for when two clauses are placed alongside each other without a coordinating conjunction such as 'and'). Although we use parataxis all the time in conversation (e.g. 'I liked the film, the music too', where the comma acts as a sort of mental dash), in written English it breeds madness and confusion. Study the next sentence:

> This may be another aspect of the tragedy of the play, Lear is not allowed to redeem himself fully.

This is trickier to resolve. If we were to supply a conjunction like 'and', 'but', or 'because', we would alter the meaning of the sentence in a way I don't think our student intends. In this case, we would be better off avoiding parataxis by reorganizing the sentence, rather than supplying a conjunction:

> Another aspect of tragedy in the play is that Lear is not allowed to redeem himself fully.

Let's consider a final example of how paratactic problems can be negotiated:

> Rodin and Balzac were similarly tenacious in character, both worked on projects that occupied them throughout their careers.

There are a few ways of getting around this ungainly construction. We can either make two halves out of it (replacing the comma with a semicolon or a full stop); we could change the comma into a dash; or we could alter 'worked' to 'working', which is the option I would choose:

> Rodin and Balzac were similarly tenacious in character, both working on projects that occupied them throughout their careers.

57

Hanging participles

'Hanging participles' (sometimes called 'dangling' participles) does not refer to a sick hobby, but a common grammatical error:

> Having read *Sense and Sensibility*, Jane Austen presents Elinor and Marianne Dashwood as two extremes . . .

The *participle clause* in this sentence is:

> Having read

and the *participle* itself:

> -ing

The problem is that we're not sure whether the participle clause relates to the reader of *Sense and Sensibility*, or to Jane Austen herself. Does the essay writer want to say that Jane Austen has read *Sense and Sensibility* and then presented the Dashwood sisters as two extremes? Or has the student read the novel and concluded that Austen presents the Dashwoods as extremes? We all know what is *meant*, of course; but that won't cut any ice with your tutor. After all, if you're doing an English degree (or for that matter any degree written in English), and can't express yourself clearly in that language, how can you expect to get good marks?

Beware the passive

ACTIVE: the dog bit the man
PASSIVE: the man was bitten (by the dog)

In passive constructions, we don't have to stipulate who is doing the action of the verb (in this case 'biting'). Consequently, when we want a statement to appear impersonal and authoritative, we often use a form of the passive. For instance:

The sample has been exhaustively tested.

One to be taken twice a day.

The government is not to be trusted to keep its election promises.

This is all very well in spoken (or medical) English, but when writing essays beware of couching everything in the passive. Especially beloved of students are constructions such as: 'it will be shown that . . .', or 'it has been suggested that . . .' Yet these tend to give an essay a rather clinical, detached air and can very quickly alienate the reader. Be more direct – shoot from the hip:

This essay shows that . . .

My discussion demonstrates that . . .

Instead of writing, as an otherwise very good student did:

This comparison *has been made* in order to allow Heathcliff's association with canine imagery *to be brought* into focus.

try the much shorter, more forceful, and no less authoritative:

I have made this comparison to draw Heathcliff's association with canine imagery into focus.

Or, if you don't feel comfortable using 'I':

This comparison draws Heathcliff's association with canine imagery into focus.

In addition to changing passive constructions into active ones, you'll see that I've also jettisoned the equally robotic 'in order to'. We are left with a sentence that is finely balanced and really quite elegant. You might, if you are feeling extra-confident and on top of your texts, cultivate a different kind of authority. How about:

I make this comparison to draw Heathcliff's association with canine imagery into focus.

This has a certain panache or swagger, and fairly exudes confidence. The stark 'I make' is bold, almost boastful, and very 'present' – and not just in terms of tense. You certainly wouldn't want to go overboard with this kind of tactic, but used sparingly it can be very effective.

Apostrophes ('s)

This first thing to note is:

it's = it is, as in 'it's a nice day'
its = possessive, as in 'to take Wordsworth's poem on its own terms' (NO apostrophe)

In academic essays, avoid using contractions like 'it's' – even when you *do* mean 'it is' or 'it has'. Write the words out in full (I know I haven't in this book, but that's different – I'm trying to appear affable and approachable). Other regular offenders in this respect are 'isn't', 'can't', and 'doesn't'.

Here are some more potential *'s* pitfalls:

Joel Harthes's reading of the poem is utterly inscrutable.

Wordsworth's and Coleridge's *Lyrical Ballads* were first published in 1798. (Both authors need *'s*)

Jane Moore's introduction is exemplary.

The two poets' gender agenda is explicit in their joint preface.

This trait is apparent in all of Jane Austen's heroines.

Writing Essays is the people's choice.

This book is yours. (NO *'s*)

> **Note:**
> 1 For plural nouns that *don't* end in s (like 'men', 'children', and 'sheep'), we add 's to indicate possession: *'the men's boat'*.
> 2 If a plural noun already ends in s (like 'boys', 'friends', or 'poets'), and we want to indicate possession, an apostrophe is required but no extra s: *'the boys' toys'*.
> 3 However, with *names* ending in s, add 's: *'Joel Harthes's theories'*.
> 4 In the fifth example above, note that it is Jane Austen, NOT Austin (no one will take your essay on *Pride and Prejudice* seriously if you can't spell its author's name).

Hyphens

She is twenty-three years old

A twenty-three-year-old man

In the twentieth century

A twentieth-century reader

But don't hyphenate adverbs ending in -*ly*:

the steadily rising tide

the wrongly accused man

the recently appointed professor

Similarly:

a mid-twentieth-century text/in the mid-twentieth century

But

an early twentieth-century text/in the early twentieth century

Who & whom

Be honest – how many of you know when to use 'who' and when to use 'whom'? You shouldn't worry if you don't have a clue: hardly any native speaker of English does. Nevertheless, the rules are quite simple. If we are referring to people rather than things, we use 'who' for *subject* relative pronouns and 'whom' for *object* relative pronouns. Calm down, I'll explain these terms. But before I do, let me remind you what subjects and objects are, and how to recognize them.

The 'subject' is the name given to the person or thing doing the action of the verb in a sentence. The 'object', on the other hand, receives the action of the verb. Study this example:

    S   V   O
    John caught the ball.

'John' is the subject because he is the one doing the action of the verb (the catching). The 'ball' is the object, because it is receiving the action of the verb (by being caught).

Get the idea? I'll move on to subject and object *relative pronouns*:

            O   S V
    That is the man *whom* I saw yesterday.
                └────┘

The relative pronoun (italicized) refers to 'man'. 'Man' is the object of the sentence, so we need to use 'whom'.

            S   V   O
    That is the man *who* sells tickets.
                └──┘

This time 'man' is the subject, so we need to use 'who'.

For a quick method of determining whether a relative pronoun is linked to the object or subject of the sentence, ask yourself if the sentence would still make sense without the pronoun? If it would, then you are dealing with an object pronoun. If not, you are looking at a subject pronoun. Consider the first example again – can you see that 'whom' is optional? Therefore it must be an object pronoun. By contrast, 'who' in the second example is necessary for the sentence to remain comprehensible, which means it must be a subject.

How does all this translate into a more academic context?

underestimate.

The relative pronoun relates to the object (Leigh Hunt), and could be left out if we chose. If we decide to keep it, however, we need to make sure we write 'whom' not 'who'.

By contrast, here is an example of the relative pronoun as subject. This time it can't be omitted:

William Cobbett was a man *who* worked hard to make himself a thorn in the establishment's side.

That & which

The next thing to agree on is when to use 'that' and when to use 'which'. You'd be surprised at how many experienced writers swap to 'which' when they feel they've used 'that' too often, or else use 'which' for plurals and 'that' for singulars. Yet the rules are quite straightforward. Although 'that' and 'which' are inter-changeable in spoken English, it is best to use 'that' to introduce *defining relative clauses*, and 'which' for *non-defining relative clauses*. I'll explain these terms for you now.

Defining relative clauses

These tell us exactly *which* person or thing is meant:

> The fish (*that*) I want is red.

Which fish? The one that I want ('ooh, ooh, ooh!'). For a slightly more academic example:

> The most accomplished early poem (*that*) Keats wrote is 'On First Looking into Chapman's Homer' (October 1816).

You can see that 'that' is an object pronoun, and can thus be left out if you wish. Be careful, though. Some tutors have a vehement aversion to students omitting relative pronouns. If your tutor doesn't have an e-mail address (or these days a personal webpage), he or she probably regards omitted relative pronouns as evidence of general cultural decline. If you suspect your tutor of being 'old-school', it would be as well to include *all* relative pronouns, irrespective of whether they are subject or object, defining or non-defining.

Non-defining relative clauses

These give extra information about the person or thing described. They are preceded by a comma (or enclosed in commas if followed by another clause, as in the next example):

> The new fish, *which* likes to swim near the surface, cost a ridiculous amount of money.

and:

> These three poems, *which* Keats wrote in the spring of 1819, represent an astounding achievement.

Whose

I'll conclude this section by clarifying how to use 'whose'. A few examples should suffice:

> This is exemplified in the paintings of Mitchell Wainright, *whose* style after 1987 becomes more urgent and unsettling.

> John Clare, *whose* poems we have been discussing, spent much of his adult life in a mental asylum.

> Charles Lamb, *whose* sister Mary killed their mother in a bout of mental instability, was one of Britain's great essayists.

Whatever happens, don't do what an otherwise very good student did and ruin an excellent sentence by misspelling 'whose' as 'who's' (= who is):

> The heroine, *who's* character becomes increasingly dynamic in the novel, labours under a series of class stereotypes.

I have only one word to say here, and it is 'Argghhh!'

Antecedent nouns

Antecedent nouns are words to which pronouns like 'he', 'she', and 'it', and determiners like 'that' and 'which', refer back. For instance:

> In *Jane Eyre*, the eponymous <u>heroine</u> is caught in a sadistic circle of punishment and desire, and ends the novel as <u>she</u> began, subject to Rochester's moods and whims.

Here 'she' refers back to the antecedent noun 'heroine'. If there is too great a distance or too much going on grammatically between the pronoun and its antecedent – particularly when other nouns are involved – sentences quickly become confusing and may even spiral out of control:

65

In response, Herring composed a story about a little boy and a pony who wore a red ribbon, which was very well loved. He won an award for it in 1923.

Help! Which antecedent noun is connected to the relative pronoun 'who' – 'pony' or 'boy'? Who on earth is wearing the red ribbon? Is it the 'story', 'pony', or 'boy' that was well loved? And as for who won the award, and for what . . .! This sentence is a complete mess because it is impossible to tell which antecedent noun belongs to which relative pronoun.

Chaos can also arise through mismatched antecedent nouns:

The role of French sculpture was to arouse patriotism and celebrate <u>its</u> great historical figures.

Was it the role of French sculpture to celebrate great figures of French sculpture, great figures of patriotism, or great figures in French history? I ask, because things are extremely ambiguous as they stand. The ambiguity arises since 'its' needs an antecedent noun, and reaches out to 'French *sculpture*'. Yet I am sure that the student who wrote this sentence is not suggesting that the role of French sculpture was to celebrate great figures in the history of French sculpture! Rather, it is *France's* history that is meant. Clearly 'its' and 'French sculpture' are mismatched, and one of them will have to go:

The role of French sculpture was to arouse patriotism and celebrate France's great historical figures.

Oui bon! You see, grammar is actually very easy. All you need to do is read through your work and decide which combination of words expresses your meaning most accurately.

Last thoughts on pronouns

When I was writing this book, a passage in Chapter 4 caused me quite a few problems:

Although Mike's final paragraph is, on first glance at least, a 'summary' conclusion, it doesn't really summarize any argumentative processes. <u>Mike</u> was probably a little unsure himself about what his essay had demonstrated, and this shows in his conclusion.

As I had used the student's name frequently in surrounding paragraphs, I thought I ought to try and replace the underlined 'Mike' with 'he'. This produced the following:

Although Mike's final paragraph is, on first glance at least, a 'summary' conclusion, it doesn't really summarize any argumentative processes. <u>He</u> was probably a little uncertain himself about what his essay had demonstrated, and this shows in his conclusion.

Something was still wrong. To be able to link 'he' to the concept of Mike, the reader first needs to see the name 'Mike'. However, what we actually get is 'Mike's final paragraph' (where the antecedent noun is 'paragraph', not 'Mike'). Linguistically speaking, there was enough of the student in question in the noun phrase to dupe me into thinking that I could deploy 'he'. But there is a whole universe of difference between 'Mike' and 'Mike's final paragraph'. For this reason the passage read oddly – like the example about French sculpture we just looked at. In the end I had to accept that it was better to repeat the student's name after all than allow a grammatical beast to slouch into my book. Sometimes one has to compromise between stylistic elegance and grammatical propriety (although, generally speaking, elegant prose will also be grammatical prose).

I could see, but now I'm blind!

One of the first things to happen to many students when they enter an exam is that their grammatical faculties promptly jump ship. Have a look at the following passage from an English paper: see if you can separate the wheat from the chaff:

Jean Rhys wrote *Wide Sargasso Sea* in the 1960's and like *Jane Eyre* is partly autobiographical and has many references to Rhys's upbringing. Born in the West Indies but moved to England when 16 years old, Rhys encountered *Jane Eyre* and developed a particular curiosity to the character of Bertha Mason. Rhys was interested in her as she too came from the West Indies and considered the treatment of Bertha as unfair and looked upon the character sympathetically.

There is actually a fairly good piece of writing in here trying to get out; the whole thing just needs tidying up grammatically and stylistically:

Jean Rhys wrote *Wide Sargasso Sea* in the 1960s. Like Charlotte Brontë's *Jane Eyre*, Rhys's novel is partly autobiographical and contains many references to the author's own childhood. Born in the West Indies, Rhys moved to England at the age of sixteen where she first encountered *Jane Eyre*. She developed a particular interest in the figure of Bertha Mason, who in Brontë's novel arrives, like Rhys, in England from the West Indies. This shared perspective allows Rhys to look sympathetically upon the character.

OK, it might still be a little higgledy-piggledy, but it's a hundred times better than it was. We've rectified decidedly odd expressions like 'Born in the West Indies but moved to England when 16 years old' and 'she developed a particular curiosity to Bertha Mason'. We've also split the long and confusing last sentence into two more easily digestible chunks. Finally, we've picked up irritating little blunders like the superfluous apostrophe in the phrase 'in the 1960s'.

Commonly misspelled & confused words

In the age of the spel-cheker, pore speling is practtically unforgiveable. Yet the same old words still slip through the net. Here are a few that continue to cause many students (not to mention some tutors) difficulties:

analyse	principal/principle
cannot	accept/except
concede	elusive/illusive
misspell	there/their
perceive	ambiguous/ambivalent
perhaps	whether/weather
proceed	Jacobin (radical association, founded during the French Revolution, which, led by Robespierre, instituted the Reign of Terror)/Jacobite (adherent of James II after his overthrow in 1668)
surprise	
interpret	

Note:

1 **Read over** your work – best of all out loud – making sure it is grammatically coherent.
2 **Watch out** for silly 's mistakes and wrong spelling.
3 Never assume your tutor will know, or have the patience to work out, what you mean. It is your job to **make yourself clearly understood.**
4 Make sure you **say what you mean** at all times.

Chapter 6

Improving your style

Some students assume that so long as all the points they want to make are in their essay somewhere, no one will care about *how* they have been made. Unfortunately, this isn't the case. Lecturers have to negotiate large batches of essays at a time; if yours looks like it's going to be a drab, monotonic exemplar, their interest may evaporate like the morning dew. You could even find yourself being marked down – needlessly – when a few minutes spent thinking about style would have made all the difference. Your task in a written assignment is not merely to cobble together an argument, but to gain your reader's attention and *hold* it. You will only do this by making your style interesting.

If we're going to improve the way we write, we need to relearn to feel 'the fine spell of words' (Keats, *The Fall of Hyperion*). I say 'relearn', because in our childhood we experienced words as virtually physical, tangible things – can you remember actually *being* there in the stories you read as a child? Sadly we lose this ability as we grow older, through inhibition, stress, or apathy; we forget that we were – and are – capable of giving and receiving 'melodious utterance', to borrow from Keats once more. This chapter will help you to rediscover the power of words and enrich your style.

Functional stylistics: more on signposting

Signposts, you'll remember, are those little words and phrases that help readers navigate their way through an argument. Under the following sub-headings, I've listed signposts frequently found in modern criticism, indicating where they can be most advantageously deployed in your essays:

Signposts for use in introductions

In this essay, I want to examine/consider (e.g. Shakespeare's use of sub-plot, etc.)

In this essay, I address . . .

This essay seeks to disclose . . .

My discussion details . . .

My thesis proposes that . . .

In what follows, I will . . .

To introduce new points & ideas:

The following section investigates/examines/explores/considers . . .

My purpose here is to draw into sharp focus . . .

To this point I have considered . . . I now want to determine the extent to which . . .

Critic X suggests/asserts/proposes/insists/contends/argues that . . .

Continuing/developing points already made

Moreover, . . .

What is more, . . .

Further to this theme, . . .

I want to elaborate this theme by asking . . .

This proposition could be considered from a slightly different perspective . . .

For use in conclusions

To conclude, I want to . . .

Singly, these instances of X do not prove a great deal. Taken together, however, . . .

The foregoing evidence I have presented leaves little doubt that . . .

My discussion has shown that . . .

The real lesson to be learned from a study of X, is the extent to which . . .

Finally, . . .

You'll see that I've included 'I' or 'my' in several phrases, and you're perhaps worried because your teachers at A level told you never to do this. Employed judiciously, however, I/my can be very effective. They allow you to 'step out' of the essay to speak more directly to the reader, and also inject a human dimension to the discussion (remember what we said in Chapter 5 about the passive voice and the perils of clinical, robotic detachment). Finally, they show your tutor that you are confident enough to use your own voice. While you certainly don't want to introduce every point with 'I' – instead of sounding suave and knowledgeable, you could come across as 'half-baked' – you might consider using the first person in your introduction, at key junctures in your argument (where you want to strike off in a new direction, say), and in your conclusion. For an extremely effective use of I/my, where exactly the right balance is struck, look back to Jane Moore's introduction at the beginning of Chapter 1.

Developing a voice: 'melodious utterance'

While we're on the subject of useful phrases, we might pause to think about how we can make our points sound more authoritative and eloquent. For instance, instead of writing (rather obliquely), as one of my students did:

Brontë shows Heathcliff as a powerful force of nature

why not say:

Brontë *presents* Heathcliff as a powerful force of nature

Or even better:

Brontë *projects* Heathcliff as a powerful force of nature

Similarly, in place of the somewhat unimaginative:

Edmund pretends to be a loyal son to his father, Gloucester

how about trying:

Edmund *masquerades* as a loyal son to his father, Gloucester

Or even (and this is advanced stuff):

Edmund *masquerades loyalty* to his father, Gloucester

Rather than saying:

Wollstonecraft uses lots of feminine pronouns when she describes the landscape of Sweden

why not venture:

Wollstonecraft genders the Swedish landscape as feminine

or refer to Wollstonecraft's

gendering of the Swedish landscape

You'll notice that as the sentences get better they also tend to get shorter. Economical prose often has a more direct impact on the reader, and is thus more effective than long, rambling sentences. So where you might once have written:

The knight-at-arms does not seem to have much control over his environment in Keats's poem 'La Belle Dame Sans Merci' . . .

you could say:

The knight-at-arms' agency in the poem is limited.

> **Note:**
>
> *Agency* – the extent to which a character has influence over what happens in his or her narrative. For instance, when Susan Wolfson discusses Keats's life, she talks about a world 'in which his agency is slight at best' ('Keats Enters History', in *Keats and History*, ed. Nicholas Roe (Cambridge: Cambridge University Press, 1995), p. 19).

The judicious use of an idiom or two can also liven up your prose dramatically. For example:

Local signs that the president's administration was in difficulty were to be found in . . .

Bismarck's policy at this juncture *casts in bold relief* the differences between Prussia's attitude towards the northern and southern German states.

Wolsey had his *finger on the pulse of the times*.

With just a little thought you can dress up your ideas in language more persuasive and authoritative than you would normally use. Don't just think about what you say, but also about how you come across to your reader. This can make all the difference – imagine the reaction of the weary soldiers at Agincourt, if, instead of his rousing 'Once more unto the breach' address, Shakespeare's Henry V had said, 'Look, I know lots of you have been slaughtered, but I'd like to ask you to fight on for a bit, if that's alright with you, that is?'

Variety is the spice of life

Since we're concentrating on style, let me draw your attention to the concept of 'elegant variation'. Essentially, this just means finding different ways to say the same thing to prevent your reader from falling asleep. Imagine you are writing an essay on Disraeli's government; you'll probably have occasion to use the phrase 'Disraeli's government' several times. But if you refer repeatedly to 'Disraeli's government', 'Disraeli's government' could very quickly become a topic of some not inconsiderable tedium. You might try a few alternative phrases for signalling this particular 'prime minister's regime'. Why not intersperse 'Disraeli's leadership' with his 'period in office', or even his 'years of rule'. If you were feeling especially lyrical, you could venture something along the lines of:

While his hand was at the rudder, Britain's influence (waxed/ waned/stayed the same).

It's the same scenario with regard to characters in books. Let's say you are writing on the representation of women in John Keats's poem, *The Eve of St Agnes*, a romance involving two characters, Madeline and Porphyro. Rather than endlessly repeating Madeline's name, mix in some allusions to 'the poem's heroine' or the 'female protagonist'. If these phrases seem a little prosaic, you could always use Keats's own elliptical reference to Madeline as 'St Agnes's charmèd maid' (line 193).

This principle of avoiding repetition applies at every juncture of the essay. For instance, if on re-reading your work you discover that you are using the word 'quotation' too much, in phrases like:

This quotation from critic X shows that . . .

Critic X quotes critic Y to great effect

swap it for a word that has a similar meaning (i.e. a synonym), such as 'citation':

This citation from critic X shows that . . .

Critic X cites critic Y to great effect

Or even:

In the words of critic Z, . . .

Be careful not to go overboard, though. It isn't worth ending up with awkward and cumbersome circumlocutions, simply to avoid using the same term twice. That is to say, if you've just mentioned Keats's knight-at-arms, don't feel you have to search for an expression like 'the armoured lover' or 'the visored loiterer' to be able to refer to him again. Use your discretion. Remember, the last drop makes the cup run over! The most important thing is to start thinking about style, and consider your reader. Make your essay a pleasure to read – throw in a few surprises and one or two well-finished phrases. It *will* be appreciated.

Once you begin thinking of alternative ways to say things, it soon becomes second nature. The following lists only took me ten minutes or so to compile:

- *Points* can be underlined, underscored, highlighted, drawn attention to, or drawn into focus.
- *Arguments* can be detailed, determined, assessed, considered, confirmed, proposed, ventriloquized, marshalled, or rehearsed.
- *Critics* can be quoted, cited, reiterated, refuted, deferred to, demurred from, negotiated, manoeuvred around, or ignored (!)
- *You* have ideas, notions, concepts, conceptions, or suggestions.
- *Positions* can be confirmed, defended, modified, strengthened, refined, or relinquished.

STOP PRESS: three words that have become quite popular in recent criticism are 'contestation', 'discourse', and 'rhetoric'. They are generally used in the following senses:

1 'Contestation', for disagreements or arguments:

The early nineteenth century was a period of intense ideological contestation between agents of entrenched state conservatism and increasingly vocal reformers.

2 'Discourse', for ideas, political positions, dialogues:

In Cobbett's *Grammar of the English Language* (1818), particularly in his vehement rejection of rules based on Latin and Greek paradigms, we discern a radical discourse of theorized opposition to wider conservative politics.

Leigh Hunt's attacks on the Prince Regent, and on the government of the day – particularly during the suspension of Habeas Corpus in 1817 – contribute to an especially fraught period of cultural and political discourse.

3 'Rhetoric', for a mode of address, or manner of speaking:

The rhetoric of ingrained literary conservatism is apparent throughout Lockhart's reviews of Hunt and Keats in *Blackwood's Edinburgh Magazine*.

Edmund's soliloquies in *King Lear* are text-book examples of the self-justifying rhetoric of insubordination.

England's coffee houses and public houses were awash with revolutionary rhetoric in the 'Days of May'.

You might also wish to 'excavate' an argument or debate from a period of history, instead of merely uncovering it; assess the extent to which Leigh Hunt's politics were 'mapped' onto Keats's early poetry, instead of simply showing how Hunt's politics are visible in Keats's poetry (a word of warning: 'mapping' is fast becoming critical jargon); demonstrate how Austen's comic style 'modulates' rather than ranges from warm humour to dry satire; illustrate how X is not 'contingent on', instead of merely not dependent on, Y; or 'locate' a 'text' at the 'intersection' of contemporary nineteenth-century debates, rather than just placing a book in its historical context.

Get the idea?

Phrases to avoid

In the last section of this chapter, I want to alert you to some phrases that should be used sparingly, or avoided altogether. We could kick off with the following:

It can be seen that . . .

I think that . . .

In my opinion . . .

In order to do X, we first must . . .

It has been argued that . . . (unless you say *by whom*)

Ditto: Critics have argued that . . . *and* It is recognized that . . .

For most undergraduates, these constructions represent familiar and 'safe' ways of introducing points or moving on to new ones. However, they are very unimaginative, not to mention extremely vague. *Which* critic argues? *Who* does the recognizing? If you knew, you would have said so, and your tutor will immediately realize this, since by no means all university lecturers are stupid. If you want to invoke critical consensus or authority, there is simply no substitute for going to the library and reading around a subject. Then, having done the legwork, *show* that you have researched your topic: cite works of criticism, quote a pithy phrase or sentence. Which, for instance, do you think is more effective?

> It has been argued that Mary Wollstonecraft links the aesthetic subject to her environment.

or:

> As Elizabeth Bohls has recently argued, Mary Wollstonecraft gives the aesthetic subject a 'corporeal connection' to her environment (p. 160).

I'm going to assume you picked the latter. Incidentally, Bohls's discussion of Wollstonecraft is fascinating, and can be found in *Women Travel Writers and the Language of Aesthetics* (Cambridge: Cambridge University Press, 1995).

'In my opinion' is another formula you should treat with extreme caution. If you happen to be the historian Lawrence Stone or the literary critic Harold Bloom, then writing 'in my opinion' before making a point might load what you have to say with the accretions of a massy erudition developed over thousands of library hours. But coming from an undergraduate who has devoted perhaps a whole week to a particular topic, it just doesn't have quite the same ring. At best, it comes across as naive or comic; at worst, it smacks of arrogance. To be sure, this might be wholly unintentional; nevertheless, it can prejudice a reader against you. In any case, it is taken for granted that what you have written is your opinion.

On the subject of striking unfortunate tones, I often see work in which students have written something along the lines of:

> In this essay, I have decided to examine the treatment of punishment and upbringing in *Jane Eyre*.

The word 'decided' (like 'chosen' or 'elected') makes your reader feel as though he or she is supposed to be eternally grateful for having been granted the opportunity to share your thoughts on punishment and upbringing in Brontë's novel. I'm sure this is not how the above student intended to come across. Read through your work, or get a friend to do it for you. If your narrative persona is too stuffy and self-important – or by the same token, too diffident or self-deprecating (too 'Hugh Grant', if you like) – make some changes. You want to sound confident, but not arrogant; enthusiastic, but not cloying; and eloquent, without turning every second word into an adjective.

It is very easy to pitch your critical register too high. However, don't parade your ideas in contorted syntax and jargon in the mistaken belief that this will lend your essay weight and intellectual rigour, like this rather pretentious fellow did:

> After much consideration, I have chosen to examine Gerard Manley Hopkins's late sonnets with a view to expediting a hermeneutics that might account for the poet's internalization of a pleonastical mode of dialogical negotiation between himself and his creator.

This is awful – jargon-ridden, torturous, ostentatious, and loud without substance. Do not emulate. All this passage really says is that Hopkins uses a lot of words. If your argument is shallow, overly showy words will only exacerbate the situation; if your argument is impressive, the incomprehensible terminology will detract from its impact. You lose both ways. Aim for a more direct and communicative style.

Here are some more phrases you should think very carefully about before committing to paper:

Thus

Therefore

Clearly

Patently

Obviously

Thence

Whence

However

Indeed

Some of these are not bad *per se*, but tend to get terribly overused. The worst offenders are 'thus', 'therefore', 'however', and 'indeed', and I am as guilty as anybody in this respect. Indeed, it is easy to see why they are so popular since they provide a kind of argumentative shorthand. The problem is that we can be duped into thinking we have clinched a point merely because we have written 'thus' or 'clearly'. Use words of this ilk sparingly.

'On the one hand . . . On the other' is also a formula you ought to be wary of employing, because it often reads in a very stilted fashion. It's usually better just to use the second half of the phrase:

> Tennyson's later poetry can be, and often is, interpreted as a retreat into conservatism and nationalism. One thinks of such poems as the politically leaden 'Charge of the Light Brigade' and the morally and rhythmically stiff Arthuriana. On the other hand, the publication in 1850 of *In Memoriam*, a poem elegizing the poet's love for his dead friend Arthur Hallam, bears witness to the fact that the older Tennyson had lost none of his early readiness to experiment linguistically – or his capacity to unsettle.

A quick final word of advice. The soundest way of expanding your critical vocabulary and developing a feel for which phrases work best where, is to read criticism. My lists of good and bad phrases will set you off on the right track. But if you are serious about fulfilling your true potential as an essay writer, you'll need to fish out your library card from the back of the sofa, find out where the university library is, and steel yourself to fling back its dread portals. Who knows, it might not be so bad. These days, most libraries have computers with Internet connections. You can surf the cyber-breakers when things get too intense down in the stacks.

> ## Note:
>
> 1 Think about **how** you say things as much as **what** you say.
> 2 **Avoid** repetition.
> 3 Help your reader follow you by **signposting** your argument.
> 4 **Avoid** tired, overused phrases and critical clichés.
> 5 **Read criticism** to develop your critical vocabulary.

Chapter 7

Quotations, footnotes, & bibliographies

I am not exaggerating when I say that at least 90 per cent of students are spectacularly bad at organizing quotations, footnotes, and bibliographies. Yet, paradoxically, this is an area where anyone can shine. In this chapter, I show you how to develop an impressive-looking referencing system that will cover all your undergraduate needs.

Before I start, let me tell you that 'consistency' is the magic word as far as all references and bibliographical details are concerned. If you keep strictly to one system for the duration of your essay, you'll be fine. That is to say, if you start off using the abbreviation 'p.' for 'page', don't suddenly switch to 'pg.' halfway through. If you refer to a quote on p. 45 of a particular book at the beginning of your essay, then subsequent references should not be to p.45, P. 45, or even (ye gods!) P45.

Why is it so important to get your bibliographical details right? Essentially, it's a question of ambiguity; or rather, of *avoiding* ambiguity, because the whole point of giving clear, accurate references is to enable your readers to follow up for themselves any interesting books and articles mentioned in the course of your discussion. If you give the wrong date of publication, omit the author's name, or misspell a title, then it might be impossible for your readers to find the source they want. Imagine depriving someone of the joys of Edith Bunchdrop's *Collected Letters of Arthur Hogsbury, 1901–1922*, 27 vols (Charleston-upon-Piddle: Lampden Press, 1923). How would you live with yourself?

QUOTATIONS

Let's raise the curtains on quotations. I've divided this topic into 'long' and 'short', 'prose' and 'poetry', as slightly different conventions pertain in each case.

Short prose quotations

Any quotation between a word and a sentence in length should be incorporated within the main body of your essay. The following examples illustrate this:

(a) As Damian Walford Davies explains in his review of Dannie Abse's recent anthology, 'Anglo-Welsh' and 'Welsh Writing in English' are both terms used, if not always unproblematically, to describe 'a body of work written in English by poets who stand in some meaningful relation to Wales, its landscape, people and culture' (p. 64).

(b) It seems that fashion designers in the 1990s took Oscar Wilde's quip that 'being natural is simply a pose' as literally as they did cynically.[1] They were richly rewarded as customers fell over each other to buy the latest incarnation of the 'natural look'.

> **Note:** Please don't underline, embolden, or italicize quotations; I know it's tempting, but don't. OK?

Page numbers & footnote markers in short prose quotations

Unless you are quoting from something for the first time, in which case all bibliographical information belongs in a footnote, page numbers are placed in brackets at the end of a sentence *before* the full stop:

> . . . to Wales, its landscape, people and culture' (p. 64).

Or, if followed by a quote from a different page, before a comma, as in the following example:

> (c) Walford Davies draws attention to the anthology's aware-
> ness of 'issues of identity and distinctiveness' (p. 64), and
> its celebration of 'living presences and [. . .] ghosts, shades
> invoked' (p. 66).

You'll notice that I have abbreviated 'page' to 'p.' in the first example, followed by a space and the relevant page number. If the quotation runs over the page in the text you are quoting from, use 'pp.' (short for 'pages'), followed by a space and the inclusive page numbers separated by a hyphen, like so:

> (d) As Thomas Woodman notes, 'such poets also have the
> problem of distinguishing themselves from mere "prince-
> pleasers"' (pp. 46–7).

See this chapter's 'Bibliographies' section for a full reference to Woodman's article.

Observe that I've written pp. 46–7. Be as economical as you can with bibliographical details, but make sure you give enough information to avoid ambiguity. With the teens the teen digit is repeated – i.e. 113–14 rather than 113–4 – because the numbers represent single words – thirteen, fourteen, etc. Here are some more examples:

p. 1, pp. 1–2, pp. 9–10, pp. 15–16, pp. 23–4, pp. 54–63, pp. 103–7, pp. 112–13, pp. 187–8, pp. 1101–2, pp. 1453–4

Footnote markers are placed at the end of a sentence *after* the full stop:

. . . that 'being natural is simply a pose'.[1]

Long prose quotations

These are separated from the main body of the text. There are two ways of making them stand out: either keep the long quotation in 12-point, but indent it from the left margin, thus:

(e) While he was at Paris, Franz Liszt came under the influence of perhaps one of the most captivating figures in nineteenth-century music, the Italian violinist Niccolò Paganini (1782–1840). The result was immediate, as Donald J. Grout explains:

> Stimulated by Paganini's fabulous technical virtuosity, Liszt determined to accomplish similar miracles with the piano, and pushed the technique of the instrument to its furthest limits both in his own playing and in his compositions. (p. 581)

Or use smaller 10-point type, in which case you no longer need to indent the text. For instance:

(f) While he was at Paris, Franz Liszt came under the influence of perhaps one of the most captivating figures in nineteenth-century music, the Italian violinist Niccolò Paganini (1782–1840). The result was immediate, as Donald J. Grout explains:

Stimulated by Paganini's fabulous technical virtuosity, Liszt determined to accomplish similar miracles with the piano, and pushed the technique of the instrument to its furthest limits both in his own playing and in his compositions. (p. 581)

For a full reference to Grout's compendious book, see the section on 'Bibliographies' later in this chapter.

Note: Always leave one line space before and after long quotations.

Page numbers & footnote markers in long prose quotations

Footnote markers are placed *after* the full stop in both long and short quotations:

. . . in his own playing and in his compositions.[1]

Page numbers are slightly different, however. Compare examples (a) and (f): with short prose quotations incorporated in the main body of the text, page numbers are given in parentheses *before* the full stop:

From (a): . . . its landscape, people and culture' (p. 64).

With long prose citations (where a line space is left before and after), page numbers are placed in brackets *after* the full stop, like footnote markers:

From (f): . . . and pushed the technique of the instrument to its furthest limits both in his own playing and in his compositions. (p. 581)

We do this to clarify that the page reference is not part of the text being quoted. This problem does not arise with short citations, where the beginning and end of the quoted material are clearly marked by inverted commas.

Don't interrupt sentences with indented quotations

Never break a sentence in half with a long quotation. That is, never, *ever* do this:

(g) The environment has long been a global issue, as David H. Close explains,

> Environmental problems have [. . .] confronted governments with new responsibilities, and provoked conflicts either between governments and citizens, or between different branches of the political system. They have also stimulated new forms both of protest and of remedial action.[1]

and the situation looks set to become increasingly tense.

If you want to incorporate Close into your argument, you should do it like this:

(h) The environment has long been a global issue and the situation looks set to become increasingly tense, as David H. Close explains:

> Environmental problems have [. . .] confronted governments with new responsibilities, and provoked conflicts either between governments and citizens, or between different branches of the political system. They have also stimulated new forms both of protest and of remedial action.[1]

For a full reference to Close's article, see 'Bibliographies'.

Omissions

You can omit unimportant (or inconvenient) words, or even whole sentences, from any passage you are quoting from, but make sure you notify your reader by replacing the text in question with three dots in square brackets [. . .]:

Dickens populates his ill-lit, claustrophobic London backstreets with a cast of minutely observed caricatures [. . .], testament to their creator's understanding of the darker tones of human psychology.

In this case I left out ', particularly in *Oliver Twist* and *Edwin Drood*'. The technical term for three dots is an ellipsis.

Quoting poetry

If the quotation is a line or less in length, treat it like a short prose quotation:

(i) We could say that in this aspect of foreign policy, the prime minister arrived, metaphorically speaking, at the 'two roads' diverging in the 'yellow wood' described in Robert Frost's famous poem 'The Road Not Taken' (l. 7).

If the quotation runs over two lines, indicate the break with a vertical slash | or with a forward slash / if you prefer. For example: 'But oh! that deep romantic chasm which slanted | Down the green hill athwart a cedarn cover!' (Samuel Taylor Coleridge, 'Kubla Khan', ll. 12–13).

If the quotation is longer than two lines, the verse should be set out as it appears in the original source. Leave a line space before and after:

(j) In stanza one of John Keats's 'La Belle Dame Sans Merci', a chilling scene of physical and psychological desolation is painted in a few deft strokes:

> O what can ail thee, knight-at-arms,
>   Alone and palely loitering?
> The sedge has withered from the lake,
>   And no birds sing.
>   (ll. 1–4)

Note: All long verse quotations are indented from the left margin.

Giving line numbers in poetry quotations

For one line of poetry or less:

> . . . in his famous poem 'The Road Not Taken' (l. 7).

For longer quotations:

> And we are here as on a darkling plain
> Swept with confused alarms of struggle and flight,
> Where ignorant armies clash by night.
>
> (ll. 35–7)

Incidentally, these lines are from Matthew Arnold's 'Dover Beach' (1851), and in my opinion are among the most powerful written in English.

FOOTNOTES

Footnotes go at the bottom of the page. Here are some to accompany publications mentioned in this chapter; I've organized them under headings to draw your attention to stylistic differences (you should not use headings in your essays, however).

Books

[1] Donald J. Grout, *A History of Western Music*, 3rd edn (London: Dent, 1981), p. 581.

[2] *John Keats: The Complete Poems*, ed. John Barnard, 2nd edn (Harmondsworth: Penguin, 1977), p. 334.

Essays in books

[3] Thomas Woodman, '"Wanting Nothing but the Laurel": Pope and the Idea of the Laureate Poet', in *Pope: New Contexts*, ed. David Fairer (Hemel Hempstead: Harvester Wheatsheaf, 1990), pp. 46–7.

Articles

[4] David H. Close, 'Environmental Movements and the Emergence of Civil Society in Greece', *Australian Journal of Politics and History* 45/1 (1999), 52–64, at 52.

Reviews

[5] Damian Walford Davies, review of Dannie Abse, *Twentieth Century Anglo-Welsh Poetry* (1997), in *Interchange* 1 (1998), 64–70, at 64.

I don't want to worry you unduly, but all the commas and full stops belong where and *only* where I have put them. It takes a little time to check that everything has been positioned correctly, but it's worth the effort because nothing impresses like order in footnotes. If you're the sort of person who likes the front of their shoes to be in line when you put them away, or can't walk past a picture without making sure it is hanging properly, then you will have no problems with footnotes. If, on the other hand, straight things annoy you, there are difficult times ahead.

Let's look at these headings more closely.

Books

Details for books are given in the following order:

name of author, forename first, surname last, followed by a comma
title of book, italicized, followed by a comma
name of editor (if any)
edition (if any: i.e. 3rd edn)
number of volumes (if more than one)
place of publication, preceded by an opening bracket, followed by a colon
name of publisher, followed by a comma

date of publication, followed by a closing bracket, followed by a comma

page number(s) of quotation, preceded by p. (or pp.), followed by a full stop

For instance:

    [1] Donald J. Grout, *A History of Western Music*, 3rd edn (London: Dent, 1981), p. 581.

If the identity of the author is clear from the title of the book, you do not need to repeat it in the footnote:

    [2] *John Keats: The Complete Poems*, ed. John Barnard, 2nd edn (Harmondsworth: Penguin, 1977), p. 334.

If there is more than one volume, specify how many:

    [1] *The Letters of John Keats, 1814–1821*, ed. Hyder Edward Rollings, 2 vols (Cambridge: Cambridge University Press, 1958), II, p. 186.

Note:

1 '**Vols**' ('volumes'), like '**eds**' ('editors'), does not need a full stop, since 's' is the last letter of the full word. We only use full stops in abbreviations – that is, with words that do not end with their final letter, such as **ed.** ('editor' or 'edited by'), **vol.** ('volume'), or **trans**. ('translated by').

2 Never put a comma before brackets: i.e. never do this:

2 vols, (Cambridge: Cambridge University Press, 1999)

Essays in books

The correct order of information is as follows:

name of author, surname last, followed by a comma
title of essay, in inverted commas, followed by a comma
title of book, italicized, preceded by 'in'
name of editor(s), preceded by ed. (eds)
place of publication, preceded by an opening bracket, followed by
    a colon
name of publisher, followed by a comma
date of publication, followed by a closing bracket, followed by a
    comma
page number(s) of quotation, preceded by p. (or pp.), followed by
    a full stop

So, for example:

> ³ Thomas Woodman, ' "Wanting Nothing but the Laurel":
> Pope and the Idea of the Laureate Poet', in *Pope: New
> Contexts*, ed. David Fairer (Hemel Hempstead: Harvester
> Wheatsheaf, 1990), pp. 46–7.

Articles

The correct order of information is:

name of author, surname last, followed by a comma
title of article, in inverted commas, followed by a comma
title of journal, italicized
volume number
date of publication, enclosed in brackets, followed by a comma
inclusive page numbers of article, followed by a comma, followed
    by 'at'
page number(s) of quotation, followed by a full stop

The next footnote belongs to example (h). As I mentioned the
author David H. Close's name in the example, there is no need to

repeat it in the footnote. Also note that we do not put 'p.' or 'pp.' before page numbers:

> ¹ 'Environmental Movements and the Emergence of Civil Society in Greece', *Australian Journal of Politics and History* 45 (1999), 52–64, at 52.

Reviews

The order for details is:

name of reviewer, surname last, followed by a comma, followed by 'review of'
name of author of book under review, followed by a comma
title of book under review, italicized
date of publication of book, in brackets, followed by a comma, followed by 'in'
title of journal in which review appears, italicized
volume number
date of publication, enclosed in brackets, followed by a comma
(inclusive) page number(s) of review, followed by a comma, followed by 'at'
page number(s) of quotation, followed by a full stop

For instance:

> ¹ Damian Walford Davies, review of Dannie Abse, *Twentieth Century Anglo-Welsh Poetry* (1997), in *Interchange* 1 (1998), 64–70, at 64.

Referencing material found on the Internet

The Internet is an increasingly rich and versatile source for up-to-date information on a wide range of topics, and students and more experienced scholars alike are benefiting from it in the course of their research. Bibliographical references to Internet sources are constructed on the same principles as references to any other form of publication:

name of author, surname last, followed by a comma
title of article (if applicable), in inverted commas, followed by a
    comma
title of journal or book, italicized
volume number (if applicable)
date of publication, or 'no date', enclosed in brackets, followed by
    a full stop
'Available on Internet at:'
Internet address
'Last revised'
date of last revision

For example:

> Kenneth R. Johnston, 'Romantic Anti-Jacobins or Anti-Jacobin
> Romantics?', *Romanticism On the Net* 15 (August 1999).
> Available on Internet at:
> http://users.ox.ac.uk/~scat0385/antijacobin.html
> (Last revised 13/9/99)

and:

> Frank C. Bertram, 'Digressions on *Eye In The Sky*',
> *philipKdick.com* (no date). Available on Internet at:
> http://www.philipKdick.com/frank/eye1.htm (Last revised
> 7/2/99)

To find out when an electronic article was last revised, place your
cursor anywhere on the text in question (but not on graphics, as
these are treated as separate documents by the computer), and
click the right mouse button. A dialogue box will pop up. Select
'information' or 'about', and you'll be shown a list of details, in
amongst which will be the dates when your article was first
published and last revised.

OTHER THINGS YOU SHOULD KNOW ABOUT FOOTNOTES

Details of publication

The title of a book and the name of its author(s) rarely present a problem, but what about publisher's details? What – and more to the point, where – is the pertinent information? On the second or third page of all books (counting from the very beginning), there will be a list of names, addresses, and dates in tiny print. Let us take a book by Anthony Stevens and John Price, and scrutinize the problem more closely:

First published 1996
by Routledge
11 New Fetter Lane, London EC4P 4EE
Simultaneously published in the USA and Canada
by Routledge
29 West 35th Street, New York, NY 10001

OK – to work! Place of publication? London. If you are reading *Evolutionary Psychiatry* in the UK, you don't need to worry about Routledge's New York address. Publisher? Routledge. Date of publication? 1996. The complete reference should look something like this:

[1] Anthony Stevens and John Price, *Evolutionary Psychiatry: A New Beginning* (London: Routledge, 1996), p. 10.

Economy in footnotes

Footnotes are there to record what sources you used and cited during your discussion. They give readers the chance to follow up any interesting-looking articles and books for themselves (or to check that you aren't guilty of plagiarism). Footnotes are *not* there to host secondary or tertiary discussions, no matter how tempting this may seem. They are also not there to act as a dumping ground for anything not quite good enough to make it into your main text. You have to learn to let go! Be ruthless in limiting footnote space to details about books and articles.

Furthermore, wherever possible try to pare down the information you do include. For instance, if you have just mentioned an author's name in your discussion, and it is clear that you are quoting from their work again, there is no need to repeat the name in the footnote. Only repeat it if not doing so would give rise to ambiguity. A footnote for the next example would not include the author's name:

> In Grant Hoffmeyer's words, public interest in archaeology received a 'monumental boost' after the discovery of the Sutton Hoo burial site.[1]

One for the following passage would, however:

> The problem of disentangling literary influence is complicated by the fact that 'all authors write with posterity in mind' and very often disguise their tracks.[1] Indeed, as Elizabeth Hopkins goes on to say . . .

Note: Even though the above quotations occur in the middle of a sentence, footnote markers are placed after the next available full stop.

After the first footnote (more on economy)

The first time you refer to a book, provide bibliographical details in a footnote (author's name, title of book, place of publication, name of publisher, date of publication, and so on). For all *subsequent* references, you only need give the book's short title. For instance, assume we have just quoted a passage from Stevens's and Price's *Evolutionary Psychiatry: A New Beginning* (London: Routledge, 1996), and a couple of pages further on we want to make another reference. Our second footnote would simply contain the short title of the book accompanied by a page number, like so:

> ¹ *Evolutionary Psychiatry*, p. 89.

It could be, however, that a second footnote is not necessary at all. If we have a number of short quotations from this book within the space of a paragraph or two, and no references to any other publications intervene, we can simply insert the relevant page numbers parenthetically in the text:

> . . . as Anthony Stevens and John Price argue in their recent book, *Evolutionary Psychiatry: A New Beginning*.¹ Indeed, the psychopath in literary fiction is a familiar figure, and has proved attractive to many authors. It is not difficult to see why. For a start, psychopaths offer writers a great deal of narrative scope since they (psychopaths, not writers), are very often 'highly mobile, charming and charismatic' (p. 87).

What we must avoid at all cost are footnotes resembling this ungainly example:

> ⁸ Lyrical Ballads, Wordsworth and Coleridge, p. 104.
> ⁹ Lyrical Ballads, Wordsworth and Coleridge, p. 103.
> ¹⁰ Lyrical Ballads, Wordsworth and Coleridge, p. 104.
> ¹¹ Lyrical Ballads, Wordsworth and Coleridge, p. 66.

The fact that the title of the book comes before the authors, and has not been underlined, is bad enough; but even worse, behold – needless repetition! After the first short reference, the appropriate page numbers should simply have been included parenthetically in the text.

BIBLIOGRAPHIES

The bibliography lives at the end of your essay and tells your reader what books you have used while preparing your essay. In general, anything you have read, or even sniffed at, belongs in the bibliography; otherwise you lay yourself open to the charge of plagiarism. Some institutions will require you to distinguish between 'primary' and 'secondary' texts (i.e. literature and criticism); but whether you use sections or not, the principle for listing books is the same. Again, 'consistency' is our watchword.

A bibliography compiled out of books, reviews, and articles mentioned so far in this chapter would look like this:

Close, David H., 'Environmental Movements and the Emergence of Civil Society in Greece', *Australian Journal of Politics and History* 45/1 (1999), 52–64

Grout, Donald J., *A History of Western Music*, 3rd edn (London: Dent, 1981)

John Keats: The Complete Poems, ed. John Barnard, 2nd edn (Harmondsworth: Penguin, 1977)

Johnston, Kenneth R., 'Romantic Anti-Jacobins or Anti-Jacobin Romantics?', *Romanticism On the Net* 15 (August 1999). Available on Internet at: http://users.ox.ac.uk/~scat0385/antijacobin.html (Last revised 13/9/99)

Stevens, Anthony and John Price, *Evolutionary Psychiatry: A New Beginning* (London: Routledge, 1996)

Walford Davies, Damian, review of Dannie Abse, *Twentieth Century Anglo-Welsh Poetry* (1997), in *Interchange* 1 (1998), 64–70

Woodman, Thomas, '"Wanting Nothing but the Laurel": Pope and the Idea of the Laureate Poet', in *Pope: New Contexts*, ed. David Fairer (Hemel Hempstead: Harvester Wheatsheaf, 1990)

Note:

1 No full stops at the end of bibliography entries.
2 The names of any second authors are not reversed (see Stevens and Price).

> 3 Inclusive page numbers are given for articles, but not for essays in books.
> 4 In bibliographies (as opposed to footnotes) the surname of the author(s) or editor(s) precedes their forename(s): i.e. Brown, John – not John Brown.
> 5 Entries are listed alphabetically according to the author's or editor's surname.
> 6 In footnotes the *first* line of an entry is indented; with bibliographies the *second* and following lines are indented.

If you have two or more entries concerning the same author, use a 3-em dash rather than repeating his or her name:

> Stone, Lawrence, *The Crisis of the Aristocracy, 1558–1641* (Oxford: Oxford University Press, 1965)
> —— *The Family, Sex and Marriage in England, 1500–1800* (Harmondsworth: Penguin, 1979)

And that's about it. Don't lose your patience – the first few times you try to get quotations, footnotes, and bibliographies right you will undoubtedly become frustrated. Persevere – it *is* worth it, and you'll be surprised at just how quickly you get the hang of things.

> **Note:**
> 1 No essay is complete without **full bibliographical references** (i.e. footnotes and a bibliography).
> 2 **Consistency** is everything.
> 3 Although at first it is difficult to adhere rigidly to a system, you will **definitely save time** in the long run.
> 4 Footnotes might be tiresome to do, but they are impressive and **anyone** can get them right.

Chapter 8

Getting the most out of the library

When Dante sat down to write his vision of the innermost circles of hell in the *Divine Comedy*, it was probably just after a visit to the library. All too often, libraries give the impression of being uninviting museums staffed by dour custodians of books, rather than a vital support service for students or a place where magic can, and arguably should, happen. But once you understand the intricacies of the library, you might be able to see this aspect of student life in a more positive light. This chapter explains the principles of effective library management, and helps get your career as a library user off on the right foot. It also shows you how to avoid fines that require yet another loan.

The trick is to make the library work for you, not against you, and for that you need a system. Once you develop one, using the library can become . . . well, almost pleasurable. Without a system, the whole experience quickly deteriorates into a nightmare of Kafkaesque proportions. You will fall prey to students who hide the best books on the Weimar Republic upside-down in the biology section until they need them, or find long queues mysteriously forming around the computers just when you want to access the catalogues, or be forced to watch in open-mouthed despair as three librarians go off for lunch together, leaving a trainee member of staff to cope at the busiest period of the day. But it need not be so. Walk this way!

Introductory courses

Most universities and higher education institutions offer new undergraduates introductory courses on using the library. You will be taught how to search the catalogues, how to borrow books, and how to use Inter-Library Loans (if your library doesn't have the book you want, it can get it for you from another library). You might also be shown how to operate a range of more advanced bibliographical resources such as microfilm (old or rare books photographed onto tiny rolls of film and read through a magnifying viewer), and specialist search programs. These courses are very helpful and should not be missed: the sooner you get the hang of the library, the sooner you can stop wasting valuable hours queueing up at the Help Desk or bothering stray librarians for help. This is good, because librarians can be unpredictable, and are dangerous when cornered.

The library catalogues (how to find books)

The catalogues tell you precisely where the book you want to consult is shelved. They exist in two formats: electronically, and on paper. It's entirely up to you which one you use, but generally speaking you will save time if you take advantage of the computers. PCs allow a great deal of information to be collated quickly, and, best of all, without you even having to get out of your seat. They also tell you how many copies of a particular book the library holds, and how many of them are out on loan.

Using the computers

Programs designed for searching library catalogues generally work along the same lines. First you decide which catalogue you want to search (this is because your library probably has separate databases for periodicals and journals, books, manuscripts, and electronic resources such as CD-Roms). If you are not sure into which category your 'target' publication falls, there is usually an option in the program that allows you to search all catalogues simultaneously. This kind of search takes a little longer to run.

Let's assume you are looking for a book on a reading list provided by your tutor. As you already have full bibliographical details, you can do a *name/title* search. Simply enter the title of the book you want, together with the author's name, and wait for the shelf location to pop up on the screen. It'll look something like this:

PR4433.F7/T

(I'll explain what all those strange letters and numbers mean in a minute.) Name/title searches are the quickest and most accurate way of finding out where your book is shelved. When you only have *some* of the book's details, however, you'll need to perform one of the other searches:

1   title, or words from the title
2   author's name
3   subject/keywords

If you have a title, or part of a title, but no author, try the first option, *title, or words from the title*. This lists all books in the library that sound like yours, in the hope that the one you want will be among them. If, on the other hand, you have a name, but can't remember the title of the book, then the second type of search displays all the publications in the library listed under your author's name. The third search option, *subject/keywords*, makes an inventory of all the books in the library on similar things to yours. For instance, entering 'Romanticism' in this type of search would produce a chronicle of books on the subject of Romanticism, although the word itself might not appear in the titles of all, or indeed any, of those publications.

In addition, more up-to-date programs allow you to refine searches using 'switches' such as AND, OR, and *. For example, entering

> cyborgs AND androids

in a *subject/keyword* search calls up only those items in the database that have been 'tagged' by the library as being about both cyborgs *and* androids. Entering

> cyborgs OR androids

summons books on *either* topic. The * switch allows you to search for variants on a word. For instance:

> romant*

would assemble items tagged with *romanticism*, *romantic*, and *romantics*. It would find the following books, for example:

> Eve Benedict, *Women and Romantic Culture* (London: Nosuchpress, 2001)
>
> Michael Davies, *The New Romantics: The 80s Pop Revolution* (London: Nosuchpress, 2001)
>
> Edward Jones, *Romanticism and Empire* (London: Nosuchpress, 2001)

Using the card catalogues

In essence, all search programs work in the way I have described. Using the card catalogue is rather different, though. Whereas a computerized database consists of ones and zeros stored on a hard disk somewhere, the card catalogue is made up of several very heavy cabinets, each containing rows and rows of tiny drawers. On the front of every drawer is an alphabetical range. Find the one which covers your author's surname (for instance, the *Ela–Kia* drawer would hold information about books on or by George Eliot and John Keats, but not Rudyard Kipling). Open the drawer and thumb through the cards inside until you hit the desired author and book. From there on, it's simply a matter of jotting down the shelf reference – for which purpose you should always have a pen and a piece of scrap paper to hand – and trotting off to find the item in question.

OK, I've done all that! Now where's the bl**dy book?

Whether you use the computers or the card system, once you have your shelf location you are halfway to finding your book. Suppose we are looking for *Romanticism Is Really Interesting, Honest!* by Michael Jacobs, which in Brickshaw University Library (and any other library in the world that uses the same shelving system) is kept at PR4837.E9/J. Let's deal with the reference in stages, starting with the first two letters, **PR**4837.E9/J. First, we need to establish where books with shelf references beginning 'PR' are kept. Do this by consulting the library's floor plans, which should be displayed prominently. In Brickshaw, all PR books are kept on the second level. So up we go . . . puff, puff!

We're on level 2 now. I can see countless rows of bookshelves in front of me, all labelled at each end with two or three letters of the alphabet. Make your way over to the ones marked PR and we can begin working on the next part of the reference, PR**4837**.E9/J.

On the spine of every book or journal in the library, you'll find a sticky label with a shelf location printed on it. This ensures that, sooner or later, books end up back where they belong; it also means that you don't have to walk around with your head at ninety degrees, reading book titles in the forlorn hope that you'll stumble across the item you want by chance. Now the books on the PR shelves in Brickshaw are labelled 1–5000. Home in on the 4000s, and then slow down because our book can only be metres away. Keep a close eye on the labels as you move along – the 4800s will appear soon. Find the 4837s and we're almost there. Now we're looking for labels ending with .E9. There should only be a few of these, and we want the one with /J at the end – the 'J' being for Michael Jacobs. And there it is: *Romanticism Is Really Interesting, Honest!* Congratulations, you've found your first book. By working through each stage of the reference in turn, we pinpointed the precise location of our book. And that's all there is to it.

If you don't find *Romanticism Is Really Interesting, Honest!* at first, and the computers insist it *is* still in the library, somebody might have been reading it *in situ*. This means it is either lying on a table somewhere, or it has been put back carelessly. Check the books on either side of where yours *should* be, according to the catalogue, and you may still be lucky.

All this might sound terribly complicated, but it'll soon become second nature. It is a good idea to do some 'dry runs' well in advance of your first essay deadline, though.

The 'paper chase'

Libraries are woefully underfunded these days (when were they ever not?). As student numbers multiply exponentially, libraries find it increasingly difficult to provide enough copies of popular books to satisfy demand. This creates 'knock-on' problems. How can you show your tutor you've read around your subject and engaged with secondary criticism when there isn't any left on the shelves to engage with? When essay deadlines loom, a frustrating paper chase invariably ensues, in which you have to compete with all the other students on your course who want the same books as you. Fortunately, with just a little forethought, you can make things a lot easier for yourself.

At the beginning of each semester, your tutors will distribute course outlines telling you when particular books or topics will be studied. You'll also receive a list of essay questions and deadlines. Let's assume that your History seminar on the Weimar Republic is scheduled for the last week of October, and the first essay deadline is set for the end of the second week in November. Go straight to the library and borrow the most recent criticism – even if November seems a long way off. The best books on the Weimar Republic should still be sitting innocently on the shelves, blissfully unaware of what awaits them in the form of coffee rings, deface-ment, and puddles to be dropped in. You might not have time to read these books properly now, but you can flick through them, photocopying sections that seem useful. Remember to ask in your department or library about copyright regulations, though, and always fill in a copyright declaration form (your library will provide these) before photocopying. At the time this book went to press, one was allowed to photocopy, for private use, a single copy of an article from a journal and up to 5 per cent of a book (except for this one – buy your own, or be cursed forever). File these photocopies away, and you'll have them when you need them. It might sound obvious, but hardly anyone does it.

The alternative is to run around like a headless chicken the week of your essay deadline, when all the library has to offer on the Weimar Republic are a couple of dusty old books from the 1950s, and an odd-shaped thing without a cover to say what it is called or who wrote it.

Renewing/recalling books

Many universities let you check your library account via networked computers. Without even setting foot in the library you can see which books you have borrowed, which are due back, and which are already overdue. You can also renew, reserve, and recall books in this way.

While this may sound very convenient, the system is open to abuse. Rather than trudge over to the library to return books they no longer need, some unscrupulous students simply renew them by computer and then use them to prop open a window for a week or two. When an essay is due, they reserve or recall every single book in the catalogue that looks as though it might be of relevance – even though there won't possibly be time to read all these. Such antisocial behaviour means that other users don't get access to the best books. In fact, the only way to ensure that you get a fair crack of the whip is to resort to similar tactics, and that way *everybody* loses out. Only use the computers to renew books you really do still need, and be selective in those you reserve or recall.

Keeping tabs on your books

The library fine is a very democratic institution. No matter who you are, there's no escaping once its dread talons reach out for you. I remember receiving a letter from my university library, literally on the day before my graduation ceremony, informing me that unless I settled an outstanding debt of £1.50 incurred for returning a book late two years ago, no degree would be awarded me.

Now, during your time at university or college you will, or should be, borrowing and returning books on a regular basis. Some will be loaned to you for two weeks, others for only three days, or even twenty-four hours, and believe me it's very easy to lose track of when they are all due back. As fines mount up quickly, it is a good idea to keep a borrowing diary. This need only be a sheet of paper with three columns:

Short title of book	Due back	Returned?	Date
Rise and Fall of the Roman Empire	1.11.2000	✓	25.10.2000
Walking in Space for Beginners	5.11.2000		
How to Make Your First Million with Student Study Guides	17.11.2000		
I Conquered the World With My Guitar	18.11.2000		

You can see at a glance when your books are overdue. So long as you know what the current date is, nothing – in theory – can go wrong.

Past papers

University libraries store copies of examination papers from previous years. These are useful revision tools because they allow you to familiarize yourself with the sort of questions you'll face in your own exams. Some libraries now offer access to past papers as an online service.

Working in the library

Many students choose to write their essays in the library because they find the sense of solidarity with other students working there helpful and reassuring. It's also useful to have all the books you might need within easy reach. Just don't let yourself be whisked off by friends for a 'quick' coffee too often or you won't get anything done.

The library can also be a good place to revise in. But this leads me on to my next point . . .

Etiquette

The only thing worse than other people's kids are the ones that grow up to be other library users. To local rules and regulations you might add these:

Don't hog the computers.

Don't talk in areas where people are working (don't whisper either – it's equally as annoying).

Don't write in books – posterity isn't interested.*

---

* Actually, people have written in books for centuries and sometimes their marginal comments are more interesting than the books themselves. But don't get any ideas!

Don't sniff.

If you've got a cough, especially those dry, tickly ones, stay at home.

Don't wobble the table when you write.

Some parting advice

- The best (because quietest) periods to use the library are early in the morning and late in the evening. The computers will be free and there is less chance of other readers using the books you wish to consult.
- If you buy a photocopying card, keep it in your purse or wallet. There is only one thing more mentally destructive than walking to the library to do some copying and discovering that you've left your copycard at home, and that's trying to buy a replacement for it at the counter, finding out you haven't got enough money, and *then* walking home to get the old one (which you can't find).
- If your library operates a self-return system, whereby books are left in an 'unmanned' basket to be stamped later, please make use of it as it helps reduce queueing times for everyone.
- Allow yourself plenty of time when you know you need to use the library: things often take longer than you might expect. For the sake of your nerves and those of your fellow users, don't start looking for half a dozen books ten minutes before a lecture or seminar is scheduled to begin. It never works.
- Above all, remain calm. The Germans have a saying, 'in der Ruhe, liegt die Kraft'. Roughly translated, it means 'you're stronger when you're calmer'. These are good words to carry with you into the library.

> **Note:**
>
> 1 Take advantage of **courses** explaining how your library works.
> 2 Find out **where** the library catalogues are kept and **how they work** at your earliest convenience.

3 Avoid the paper chase by **thinking ahead**.
4 Keep a '**borrowing diary**'.
5 **Never underestimate** the capacity of librarians for rudeness (and don't take it to heart).

Chapter 9

Using computers & printing

Computers are great. They do games, they work out tax returns, they guide rockets to the moon. They are probably even sentient. One thing they don't do very well, however, is essays. Something they can't do at all is talk to printers in a meaningful manner. This chapter is all about helping you maximize your chances of successfully transferring your thoughts onto the computer monitor, and ultimately from there onto pristine sheets of A4.

Why use computers?

With large rises in student numbers, marking loads have increased exponentially over recent years. One consequence of this is that more tutors expect essays to be typed so that they can be read easily and quickly. This might sound like a lot of effort, but it need not be, as I will explain. Besides, typing essays has been absolutely standard practice in the

USA for twenty-five years. It is worth putting some thought into presentation; if your essay is 'borderline' (that is, if it falls between two grades), then good presentation might just make the difference between receiving the lower and higher mark.

There are a number of simple conventions that apply to word-processed essays, such as double-spacing and using 12-point, clear, unfussy fonts – we'll discuss these in detail. Also in this chapter: how to survive the print-out. Printing is the great student *bête noire*. The basic rule is, anything that can go wrong will go wrong, and at the worst possible time. Cringe as line-breaks slip off the bottom of the page before your eyes; sigh as printing cartridges run out at the crucial moment; weep as special characters disappear into the void, or print out as garbage, even though they look fine on the screen. This section provides you with an SOP (Standard Operating Procedure) to ensure printing goes smoothly and on time, every time.

Word-processing

As I said, these days tutors more or less expect you to type up your work. Although some students still use typewriters, this seems a little perverse in the age of the PC (personal computer). And if you don't have a PC at home, virtually all universities in the country have computer clusters (rooms filled with machines for your use). When you register as a new student at your institution, you'll be given an ID-code that allows you to 'log on' to your institution's computers. You'll probably get an e-mail address at the same time, which is important because e-mail opens up wonderful new dimensions in your life.

You might think that working with computers and having creative thoughts are antagonistic notions. You'd be wrong, though. There probably wasn't a single novel published last year that wasn't composed from start to finish on a word processor. I know that we all love the image of the Beat novelist Jack Kerouac hammering away on an old typewriter in his cold-water apartment. But those days are gone. If Kerouac were writing today, he'd be using a PC. Actually, even then, Kerouac used to tape sheets of paper together to create long, continuous rolls; he fed these through his typewriter because he didn't want to have to break his train of thought to change paper. Imagine how the endless blank screens of a word processor would have appealed to him . . .

> Yeah! Sailing the crazy gone expanses of white on a no longer lugubrious voyage through riots of radiant ideas; suddenly I found myself in LA, with zoot-suited maestros of jazz pulling on my lapels.

But I digress. To return to your institution's computing provision: if your university or college runs training courses teaching you how to use networked PCs (interconnected computers that share a printer), then make the most of the opportunity. Even if you think you already know lots about the subject, it is worth attending these courses since there are often a few logging-on procedures to be clarified that are specific to your institution, and it is best to get someone to show you how to do it right at the beginning, rather than pestering a friend the day before your (and their) first essay is due in. Also, these courses usually teach you how to use word-processing packages, which is useful because, although most word-processing programs these days work along the same principles, or are in any case fairly intuitive, the sheer number of tasks they can perform means it's easy to get lost. Do yourself and your tutor a favour by finding out how to use the computers and writing software well in advance of the first essay deadline.

On these courses you'll also be shown how to enter cyberspace and use the Internet. Woo-hoo!

In the old days, when computer screens could only do green or orange, took about ten minutes to boot up, and would only create footnotes for people with Ph.D.s in astro-science, tutors were grateful for anything that looked like it had been waved anywhere near a PC. The fact that page numbers were scribbled on by hand afterwards, and the bottom half of the last line of every page was missing, did not matter. Tutors were grateful for what they could get. These days, things are a little different. You want a footnote, you go to *Insert → Footnote*. (Obviously this depends a little on your word-processing package, but they tend to be quite similar in this respect.) You want page numbers, you go to *Insert → Page numbers*. Huzah!

Except, of course, that it's not always that simple. Often, for no apparent reason whatsoever, *Insert → Footnote* suddenly means 'change everything into a tiny font, and junk the last half hour's work'. And that is why, before I tell you anything about formatting and presenting your essay, I'm going to tell you how to save it.

Saving your work

SAVE YOUR WORK AT REGULAR INTERVALS!!!

Stare at these words for a minute without blinking. I want them burned into your retinas. Every ten minutes or so you should 'quick save' your work onto the computer's hard drive. Go to the pull-down menus at the top of the screen, and click on *File → Save* (or use the *Save* icon). The computer will do the rest. Do this manually – don't trust the program's 'autosave' function. If the computer is temperamental, this is the first function to stop working (without telling you it has stopped working).

The next security measure is to buy a floppy disk (3½ inches) – they cost about fifty pence, for goodness sake. Stick it in your floppy drive, and after each session on the computer make a back-up copy of your work. You do that by going to the pull-down menus at the top of the screen and choosing: *File → Save as*. In the relevant field give your file a name, such as 'essay1.doc'; finally, go to the *Save in* field and click on 'a:'.

Terminology note:

ǀ **Fields** are oblong spaces containing a flashing vertical line where you enter instructions for the computer. They look like this:

ǀ

> 2 'a:' is the letter usually given to designate the floppy disk drive. It is worth mentioning that before long 3½-inch disks will probably have been entirely replaced by rewritable CDs and DVDs, which are much faster and can hold a great deal more information.

OK. Now click on the *Save* button and marvel as the floppy drive grinds away for a few seconds and your essay is transferred as a series of ones and zeros onto your disk. Keep this disk safe, and don't get it wet.

All this might seem obvious, but in my time as a lecturer I have had to pretend to listen sympathetically to so many desperately unhappy students who didn't have a back-up copy of their essay when their computer crashed. Of course you can't say 'Make a back-up next time, fool!' to paying students, especially not those teetering on the edge of a nervous breakdown. But really, there is no excuse. Remember, don't trust your computer. It lives for the moment when it can crash and do the most possible damage in terms of your grades and your psychological well-being. It watches you from behind the screen, willing you not to save your work. It feeds off your misery. But its power grows weak every time you hit the save button.

I hope that my point about saving your work has been taken. If you get caught out now, there is nothing anyone can do for you.

Formatting

Now let's consider how to present your work to its best effect. The technical word is 'formatting', and it's easier than you might think – as long as you stick to a few golden rules:

1 Keep it simple.
2 Make it easy to read.
3 Be consistent.

I'll explain what I mean in the following sub-sections.

Fonts

By 'keeping it simple', I mean don't mix lots of different fonts together. Your tutor won't be impressed by weird script or fancy swirls, no matter how much fun they are to play around with. Stay with a single font that is clearly legible. It's a good idea to use a Roman font such as Times or Sabon (the font you're reading now), but you might also consider using Arial or Courier.

Font size

Set your font size to 12-point (11-point if you're using Arial, as for some reason this typeface seems to be bigger than others). 12-point is ideal for normal prose in essays printed on A4 sheets of paper. Just type '12' in the field, and the job's a good 'un. For indented quotations, you might consider using 10-point, as I discussed in Chapter 7.

Using bold & italics

If you want a piece of text to stand out, highlight the words in question with your mouse, and click on the 'bold' button at the top of the screen (the words will then become **thicker and blacker**); or highlight the words and click on the 'italic' or '*I*' button (the words will then become *thinner and slant to the right*). However, use these functions sparingly. The only time you need to have recourse to italics is when you write titles of books and journals or, *very* rarely, to emphasize a word (as I have just done). The only time you might consider using bold type is for the title of your essay. Never embolden or italicize quotations. Keep it simple – as with so much in life, less is very often more.

Finally, be consistent. If you started off by italicizing the titles of books and journals, don't suddenly begin underlining them. If you've used 10-point for indented quotations, don't suddenly change to 12-point. If you started out by indenting the first line of new paragraphs, don't suddenly stop doing it.

Pagination

Printed page numbers look much better than ones added by hand afterwards, so as soon as you start your new file, go to *Insert →* *Page numbers*. It doesn't really matter where you position the numbers, but personally I prefer to use the top right-hand corner of the page. Remember, don't number your cover sheet, if you have one.

Footnotes or endnotes?

Again, it doesn't really matter which you use. Footnotes have the great advantage of appearing directly beneath the point in the text to which they refer. This means the reader doesn't have to flick to the back of the essay all the time, which makes footnotes very user-friendly. On the other hand, if you put all your bibliographical details at the back of the essay, the reader isn't constantly distracted from the main argument by secondary information. In my opinion, however, footnotes have the edge over endnotes because they are visually more effective, and lend your essay a sense of weighty authority.

Margins

Leave generous margins for your tutor to inscribe all his or her pearls of wisdom. I would recommend 3.5 cm (1½ inches) for the left margin, and 3 cm (1¼ inches) for the right-hand one.

Spacing

Double-space your work – this gives your tutor more room to scribble comments, make corrections, or re-jig sentences. You set the essay to double-spacing in the following way. First, highlight the whole of your document (some programs let you perform this quickly by holding down the 'control' key on the bottom left of the keyboard and pressing '5' in the number pad on the right). Once everything is highlighted, go to the pull-down menus at the top of the screen. Click on *Format → Paragraph → Line spacing*, and choose 'double'. Single-spaced text (from William Wordsworth's 1800 Preface to *Lyrical Ballads*) looks like this:

> Low and rustic life was generally chosen because in that situation the essential passions of the heart find a better soil in which they can attain their maturity, are less under restraint, and speak a plainer and more emphatic language; because in that situation our elementary feelings exist in a state of greater simplicity and consequently may be more accurately contemplated and forcibly communicated.

One-and-a-half-times looks like this:

> Low and rustic life was generally chosen because in that situation the essential passions of the heart find a better soil in which they can attain their maturity, are less under restraint, and speak a plainer and more emphatic language; because in that situation our elementary feelings exist in a state of greater simplicity and consequently may be more accurately contemplated and forcibly communicated.

And double-spaced text looks like this:

> Low and rustic life was generally chosen because in that situation the essential passions of the heart find a better soil in which they can attain their maturity, are less under restraint, and speak a plainer and more emphatic language; because in that situation our elementary feelings exist in a state of greater simplicity and consequently may be more accurately contemplated and forcibly communicated.

Justification

You'll see that the lines in the first quotation from Wordsworth's Preface end unevenly down the right-hand side. This is because I did not 'justify' the passage. The other two paragraphs have been justified and are thus even. You'll find this function in *Format* → *Paragraph*, or as an icon on the top of the screen. It is up to you whether you present your work justified or unjustified.

Finally, before I talk about the perils of printing, let me remind you to leave one line free before and after indented quotations, as I have done with all of the above extracts from Wordsworth (see Chapter 7 for more information on quotations).

Proof-reading & draft print-outs

Word-processing packages are powerful and effective tools when it comes to editing. They allow you to cut and paste to your heart's content, alter individual words or whole sections, and play around with formatting options. They even check your grammar for you if you let them (although, in my experience, grammar-checkers are fairly useless for academic purposes). However, you should not expect to go straight from the 'on screen' version of your essay to the final print-out. The reason for this is that you only really get an accurate impression of how your work reads once it is on paper – i.e. in the form in which your tutor is going to receive it. Moreover, it is extremely difficult to catch typos (typographical errors) on screen. Be prepared to print off one or two draft versions of your essay, and read through them carefully.

Try to gauge how your essay will sound to your tutor. If you have time, put your work aside for a few days before the final editing session. Casting a cold eye (to borrow from Yeats) over your work often enables you to spot things you might otherwise miss. In the eighteenth century, Dr Johnson even recommended that all 'finished' compositions be locked away in a drawer for seven years! If they still seemed good after that time, they might then, and only then, be considered for publication. You may not have seven years, but you can certainly read through your essay, underlining any bits that seem odd, badly phrased, or just plain bonkers.

Mark any errors or improvements with a red pen, then go back to the computer and make the necessary changes.

The final print-out

The best advice I can offer here is to allow yourself a whole day just for printing the finished version of your essay – things invariably go wrong. When Shakespeare wrote 'Mischief, thou art afoot!' in *Julius Caesar*, he could have had the final print-out in mind. Quite aside from problems beyond your control – like the printer breaking down or running out of toner when there's no one at the Help Desk, or boatloads of students with similar deadlines to yours jamming the printer's queueing system – you'll also start noticing lots of hitherto unseen errors in your work. This might be down to wayward formatting or spelling mistakes (don't be too proud to use the spell-checker!); or it might be a case of your printer suddenly not recognizing special characters such as umlauts (ä, ö, ü) or other weird and wonderful symbols, and producing them as squares or triangles, or even – and this is particularly bitter – smiling faces ☺.

Whatever the nature of the problem, be prepared for the fact that there will be problems, and leave enough time to cater for all eventualities. The day before you're supposed to hand in your work, arrive at the computer cluster bright and early to make one last draft print-out. Then, armed with a red pen, go off and read through it with a cup of coffee. Once you've marked or underlined all your mistakes, enter the corrections into the computer and **PRESS SAVE**. Scroll through your essay, making sure that you don't have half a quote on one page, and the other half on the next, and when you are satisfied make a second print-out; and then repeat the whole 'proof-reading' procedure.

Don't become obsessive, though. Your university printing allowance will probably be small, and after a certain number of free pages you'll have to pay for extra ones yourself. Don't print your whole essay out again just because you've written 'this passage registers the author's anxiety' where you think 'this passage *records* the author's anxiety' would read better.

Handing in your essay

I'll end this chapter with some advice on what to do with the loose leaves that arrive in the print tray. Let's imagine you've just collected your essay, and the pages are still warm. You flick through it again – you've used Times Roman 12-point, you've double-spaced the text, you've left a line before and after indented quotations, you've italicized titles of books and journals. It looks good – no, it looks great! So why is it that at this stage many students think to themselves: 'I bet it'd look even better stuffed into a plastic sleeve'? Plastic sleeves belong right up there with exam invigilation duties on any lecturer's hate list. It's a devil of a job to get an essay out of a plastic sleeve, and as for getting it back in . . .

The best way to present an essay is simply to put a staple in the top left-hand corner. Don't even bother with a separate cover sheet for the title. First it's a waste of paper, and secondly it looks too precious. Aim for a more modernist approach, with form and function as your watchwords. An essay is just what it is – not a piece of art, not a portfolio, not a multimedia show – merely sheets of A4 with words on them. Its function is to be read, so make sure that as little stands in the way of this as possible. No plastic sleeve, no cover sheet, no frills, just a clearly presented essay.

And before your tutor even reads a word, you're on course for a first.

Note:

1 **Typed essays** can be **read more easily**. This will make your tutor better-disposed towards you.
2 Get your **log-in ID** and try it out at the first opportunity.

---

3 **Take advantage of courses** introducing you to your institution's computing provision.
4 **Start as you mean to go on** – get that first essay typed up.
5 Leave **plenty of time** for the final print-out.
6 **Save** your work at regular intervals.
7 **Save** your work at regular intervals.
8 **Save** your work at regular intervals. (Get the idea?)

Chapter 10

How to write exam essays

The exam essay differs from the coursework assignment, both in terms of how it is written and marked. That it is written differently should be fairly obvious. In an exam you can't mull things over at leisure, root around in the library, or type up your thoughts neatly. Instead you have two hours or so in which to write like the proverbial clappers. But the exam essay also tends to be marked differently. By that I mean lecturers these days have a terrible time of things in the exam period, when they face tsunami-sized waves of answer booklets, each containing two or three separate essays. One should appreciate that it is very difficult for lecturers to spend as long scrutinizing individual pieces of work as they would like to in an ideal world.

That is not to say that exam essays are not graded properly or fairly. On the contrary. It is just that different factors come into play when they are assessed. For instance, when markers read exam essays they tend to look for readily recognizable 'identifiers' of standard to help them arrive at a grade swiftly. Now just imagine someone were to tell you what these were – wouldn't it make your life easier?

But let's not put the cart before the horse. We'd better start off by discussing the weeks leading up to the exam.

Preparation

There *is* such a thing as 'over-preparation'. The concept is not just a myth put about by students who prefer to study the effects of alcohol consumption on the human body, using themselves as control subjects, rather than revise fiscal policy in the court of Henry VIII. 'Over-preparation' is a problem you need to take seriously. One of the worst things you can do in your revision period is do too much. It is entirely counter-productive. Your body just goes into a state of permanent panic and you can't revise properly. Then, when you are not revising properly, you get panicky, and a vicious circle forms.

A successful programme of revision reflects the fact that periods of doing nothing at all are as important as those spent in intense study. I would go so far as to say that one does not work properly without the other. Think of it as the Yin and the Yang. Rather than cramming every minute of the day, draw up a loose study schedule that reflects this philosophy of harmony and balance. Try working for two hours in the morning (between 9 and 12), two in the afternoon (between 1 and 4), and two in the evening (between 5 and 8), and see what happens. What you do in the rest of the time is up to you, but don't feel that you can't go out and relax. In my experience, students who best fulfil their potential in exams are those who manage to retain a sense of perspective and humour. Go out for a drink – take in a movie. The thought of a reward in the evening acts as an incentive to work hard during the day.

Everyone revises differently, of course. If you already have a tried and tested method of revision, why change it? If it ain't broke, don't fix it, as the old adage goes. On the other hand, preparing for a degree is not the same as revising for GCSEs or A levels. At school the emphasis was on showing how much you could *remember*. In higher education, it is all about showing how much you can *think*. And in order to think, you need to be relaxed – which you can't be if you are desperately cramming all the time.

It all comes down to common sense. If you can't sleep, or are suffering from constant headaches, perhaps you are trying to do too much (of course, there is always the possibility that you are seriously ill and should see a doctor at once).

To reiterate: there is no right or wrong way to prepare for examinations. As I keep saying, there are many ways to skin a cat. There are some common pitfalls you would do well to avoid, however. To begin with, many students spend weeks memorizing coursework essays verbatim in the hope that they will be able to regurgitate them in the examination. You are unlikely to live long and prosper with this approach. Apart from the likelihood of infringing the rubric (the rules of the exam) by repeating work already submitted, you will almost certainly end up with a second-hand essay that won't light any examiner's fire. It's much better to spend some time developing a sound framework for writing exam essays. You can then build a discussion of *any* subject on this, rather than banking on 'your' topic coming up. Learning essays verbatim might work at A level, but it rarely produces good results at degree level. (If you are an A-level student reading this, however, you would also do well to show that you can actually think in exams, rather than merely regurgitate.)

Writing the exam essay

Earlier I mentioned that examiners look for certain 'identifiers' in exam essays to provide a rough indication of standard. For instance, if on the initial 'skim through' an essay displays evidence of a developed critical vocabulary, has clearly visible 'signposts', and shows some engagement with the critical debate (a few names and quotations), then an examiner will automatically be thinking in terms of awarding at least a 2,i grade. When the essay is read more carefully, and perhaps does not quite live up to expectations, this initial impression lingers and can be of great help to you.

Conversely, if no such identifiers are apparent, even if your ideas are good you will be battling against a pre-formed opinion that your essay is a 2,ii piece of work; pre-formed because examiners know from experience that badly signposted essays, which lack a sophisticated critical vocabulary, generally turn out to be of 2,ii standard.

Don't misunderstand me; I'm not suggesting that if you usually get 2,ii marks for your coursework you can somehow 'trick' your examiner into thinking you are a 2,i student just by including a few 2,i identifiers in your work. Not exactly. But you can certainly load the dice in your favour. After all, examiners normally mark 'blind' (that is, without knowing whose script they are reading). If the examiner doesn't know who you are, then you are free to be anyone you like. Put on a disguise – don an intellectual mask. You don't need to feel like a fraud, because if your essay contains 2,i or first-class identifiers, then, for the purposes of the examiner, you *are* a 2,i or first-class student. Where's the difference? As a wise person once said (I think it was Gene Hackman in Clint Eastwood's classic film, *The Unforgiven*): 'If it walks like a duck and quacks like a duck, chances are it's a duck!'

Anyway, to return to our disguise metaphor, let's open the dressing-up box and put something on.

Positive & negative identifiers

A good exam essay is the result of a combination of various factors, and sometimes it's very hard even for tutors to say *exactly* why it is good. However, the following elements can usually be found in the best scripts somewhere, so make sure they appear in yours:

- a clear, bold statement of aims in the introduction
- a sustained sense of purpose
- signposts or an easily recognizable narrative thread to help the reader through the argument
- developed critical vocabulary
- good grammar

- a distinct 'voice' or personality
- evidence of engagement with the critical debate
- "Factor X" (what we might term 'panache')

I call these elements *positive* identifiers. By the same token, we could also enumerate *negative* identifiers:

- a loose or rambling introduction
- no clear sense of purpose
- few or no signposts to guide the reader through the argument
- very basic, undeveloped vocabulary
- no evidence that any critical works have been read
- plot-driven argument/lots of paraphrase
- no "Factor X"

Handwriting

Before I consider each of these points in turn, I want to say something briefly about handwriting. Whereas personally I do not believe that handwriting is linked to character or ability (you ought to see mine!), one could probably argue with some justification that an elegant hand impresses examiners more than bubbly letters or prototype. Without suggesting that you change your handwriting, there are a few tricks you might try. Perhaps the simplest is to swap from light-blue ink to black, as this gives an impression of authority. Many examiners are human beings and are thus vulnerable to psychological 'nudges' when they mark. If black ink helps create an aura of being in control, why not give it a go?

Remember that your handwriting is the interface between you and your reader. A barely legible paper will not do you any favours. If examiners wanted to spend their time deciphering hieroglyphics, they would move to Egypt and study the pyramids.

So let's talk about positive identifiers in more detail.

Positive identifiers

A clear, bold statement of aims in the introduction

Much of what I said in Chapter 1 applies here. As with a piece of coursework, it is vital in your exam that your reader gains an immediate sense of what it is you are seeking to discuss. Your opening paragraph must be decisive, internally coherent, and pithy (see Chapter 1 for practical examples). Try to excite the examiner's interest – make your script stand up and shout 'Here I am!', to distinguish it from the hundreds of others he or she will be reading within the space of a week or two.

Before you even begin your introduction, sketch out a brief plan of the essay you want to write. You can do this on the inside cover of your answer booklet. The plan does not have to be neat; just jot down the key ideas you want to include in your discussion. Once you have done this, you'll have a better sense of what your essay is going to be about. Perhaps you don't know precisely where your argument is going to end up, but this needn't be a bad thing. Actually, it can be very liberating to give your thoughts some free rein in an exam to lead you into places where you might not otherwise go.

We come then to the first sentence proper. Writing this is one of the hardest things you will ever have to do in your life; and for this reason it is useful to have a ready formula to hand, such as:

In this essay, I want to discuss . . .

This essay considers the . . .

The following discussion seeks to draw into focus . . .

These phrases might seem a little abrupt, and if you had time to fashion a more elegant opening gambit you might well come up with something better. But under exam conditions, such 'old faithfuls' can save a lot of time and have the additional advantage of taking you straight into your argument without any waffle. There is nothing worse than an introduction that meanders around haplessly, waiting for a point to emerge as if by magic. I once read an exam essay from a student who wanted to explore the treatment of women in *Paradise Lost* (John Milton's epic poem telling the story of humanity's Fall and subsequent expulsion from the Garden of Eden). The essay began:

> John Milton was born in 1608 and died in 1674. He went blind towards the end of his life and worked as a propagandist for the King. He was very cruel to his daughters, who copied out his poetry for him as he couldn't see to do it himself. *Paradise Lost*, Milton's magnum opus, was written in 1667. It was implicated in the struggles leading up to the Civil War in England, and although Milton worked for the monarchy, the rebel Satan receives a much more sympathetic treatment than God, who could be identified with the crown. In the following argument, I want to discuss the figure of Eve, asking to what extent Milton treats her sympathetically.

Quite apart from the rather noticeable *non sequitur* in the second sentence (what has going blind got to do with working as a propagandist for the King?), the whole introduction is little more than a barely connected sequence of points that eventually alights on the figure of Eve. I can imagine what must have happened. In desperation, this candidate wrote down everything he or she could remember about Milton in the hope that an argument would materialize. Unfortunately, the essay remained unfocused and received a low grade.

Much better is the following introduction from a History student who wrote on Germany after the fall of the Berlin Wall:

> In November 1989, after a period in which Communism underwent a radical and far-reaching change from within, the wall dividing Berlin fell. Although global news footage presented the event as an example of 'people power', the decision not to turn back the crowds demanding reform had probably been made some time before, and behind closed doors. The mood of exuberance only survived the demise of the wall for a short while; by the early 1990s a grim sense of reality had

settled as parity between the former eastern states and the rest of Germany seemed a long way off. In this essay, I want to explore the difficulties faced by citizens of the former DDR in the newly unified Germany.

This is impressive, especially when we consider it was written under exam conditions: there is a distinct narrative, each sentence follows on logically and coherently from the last, there is a clear statement of aims, and the passage contains some very good writing. Notice how this student has not always taken the obvious choice. The Berlin Wall becomes 'the wall dividing Berlin'; I also like 'mood of exuberance' (with its pleasing internal rhyme), and the ominous, if rather histrionic, 'a grim sense of reality had settled'. This student has paused to think about how best to clothe ideas in language, rather than simply pouring them out higgledy-piggledy. As I always tell my tutees, a single idea expressed felicitously is better than ten that are badly communicated and don't come across.

A sustained sense of purpose

Resist the temptation in examinations to spew out everything you can remember from lectures and seminars, as this only leads to incoherent work. A good discussion is focused and relevant; it is much better to pare things down to a few main points and explore these in detail, than skim through lots of disconnected ideas. Your tutor is interested in quality, not quantity. Four sides of A4 per essay are ample (assuming you don't write three or four words to a line). As a matter of fact, anything more than that often proves counter-productive. At any rate, the little tag you are given to join two answer booklets together in exams is an object of loathing for markers, and prompts their autonomic nervous systems to twitch in despair whenever one is seen.

Always keep your main point (the one to which you return in your conclusion) in the reader's field of vision. Compare the following two examples from our question on *Paradise Lost*. Both students want to introduce new ideas into their discussion:

1 I now want to turn my attention to Satan's temptation of Eve beneath the Tree of Knowledge . . .

2 <u>If Milton's treatment of his female protagonist up to this point has been at best tolerant,</u> in the episode where Satan tempts Eve by the Tree of Knowledge a whole range of negative stereotypes emerge . . .

Look at the underlined section in the second example. At the same time as the new point is being introduced, the reader is reminded what this particular essay has set out to do: namely, explore Milton's treatment of Eve in his epic poem. If you keep your 'target' point visible, linking back to it at salient points, your discussion will appear coherent and purposeful.

Finally, show the examiner that you are in control of your material and that you have succeeded in imposing order and structure on it. A tightly knit, well-marshalled argument never fails to impress in an exam essay, so don't allow yourself to get side-tracked. Whereas with coursework you might have time and space to follow interesting-looking trails off into the strawberry plants, under exam conditions you need to be succinct and to the point.

Signposts to help the reader through the argument

The next positive identifier goes hand in hand with the one I have just discussed. To maintain a sense of purpose and order in your discussion, you need to let the reader know what is going on at every juncture. If you are about to introduce a new point, or connect an old one to a new one, then say so – it is very reassuring from the reader's perspective, and helps give the impression that you know exactly what you are doing (even if you don't).

For example, when you introduce a new point you might use the opportunity to take stock of what you have achieved so far in your essay (WARNING: don't overuse this particular device):

To this point I have explored the interaction of X and Y; I now want to ask to what extent Y can be considered as . . .

Or you might be more prosaic, as this student was to considerable effect:

> As we have seen, Chancellor Konrad's right-wing government had a far from satisfactory policy towards ethnic minorities living in Germany. However, with the hand-over of power to Schiller's purportedly left-of-centre party, things only changed slowly, if at all, as I now wish to discuss.

Refer to Chapters 3 and 6 for more on good signposting.

Developed critical vocabulary

The best way to expand your critical vocabulary is to read criticism. Keep a notepad to hand when you read so that you can jot down useful terms and phrases. This is precisely what critics do: a decade ago, no one 'mapped' the politics of a period onto anything (thank goodness!) – now *everyone* does it. See Chapter 6 for more on developing a sophisticated critical vocabulary.

Good grammar

It goes without saying that first-class work must be grammatical (see Chapter 5). Make sure you leave yourself enough time at the end of the exam to read through your work, checking that everything makes sense. If your sentences seem to be saying something other than you intend, the chances are that the problem lies with bad grammar. Although you don't want to keep correcting your script until it resembles one of Beethoven's autograph scores – covered in blotches, with whole sections etched out into oblivion – a small amount of tinkering could make a lot of difference.

A distinct 'voice' or personality

It can take a whole degree course to develop a critical voice. However, a few judiciously placed personal interjections, such as 'I want to consider . . .' or 'in my essay I wish to explore . . .', can give the impression that you're further down this road than you may in reality be. Avoid overusing passive constructions (e.g. 'in this essay it will be shown . . .'), as it makes you sound like a Cylon from *Battlestar Galactica*. You can inject a lot of life into an essay just by reminding the reader every so often of the fact that there is a personality behind the discussion. I talk more about 'finding your voice' in Chapter 6.

Evidence of engagement with the critical debate

Students often ask me 'Should we use quotations in exams?' and I always reply, in my best John Wayne voice, 'Hell, yeah!' If you want to talk about literature, you have to be able to draw on examples, otherwise everything becomes terribly hypothetical and detached. The same goes for referring to critics. Naturally, you don't want to cite reams of Professor Bigcheese or be overly deferent to Dr Internationalreputation. However, you do need to prove to your examiner that you have done more in your studies than simply scribble 'Push Button To Abort Lecture' on auditorium armrests. An essay devoid of reference to any criticism whatsoever will have to do something extraordinary to earn more than a low 2,ii mark.

There are good reasons for expecting you to show that you have interacted with recent criticism. To begin with, if you haven't read around your subject, you run the risk of spending an hour re-inventing the wheel, and this is so tiresome to read. What's more, you ought to know what the current state of play is in your area. Just imagine a medical student trying to write a paper on organ transplant without having read anything written on the subject in the last twenty years. You would hope – indeed *expect* – that they fail their exams, wouldn't you? At the very least, you'd hope never to find yourself staring up at that particular individual from an operating table. So why should students of the humanities be surprised when they are marked down for not having read any critical works?

OK, you won't be expected to transplant anyone's organs with a humanities degree. On the other hand, you are dealing with ideas in your essays, and ideas can change the world.

I realize that it can be difficult to remember a critic's exact words. But even if you have only retained a broad sense of the quotation, stick it between two sets of inverted commas, and give the title of the book you think you remember having seen it in. Who's going to go to the library and check up on you? It's more important that you give the *impression* of being *au fait* with your material than agonizing over questions of bibliographical accuracy.

Remember, a quote or two always lends your opinions a sense of authority. Which looks better?

> Keats's first year's work as a poet owes much to his literary mentor, Leigh Hunt.

Or:

> Keats's first year's work as a poet owes much to his literary mentor, Leigh Hunt. As Jeffrey N. Cox says, 'Keats's early work . . . insists upon his links to Hunt' (p. 89).

'Nuff said. Incidentally, I *do* remember where I read this quote – in Cox's book, *Poetry and Politics in the Cockney School* (Cambridge: Cambridge University Press, 1998). And very good it is, too.

"Factor X"

This is that indefinable something, that elusive *je ne sais quoi* that makes an essay stand out from the others around it. Perhaps the best word to describe it is 'panache' or 'flair', since "Factor X" is more of an attitude than anything else. It's a little like self-confidence: some days you have it, some days you don't. Your best chance of finding "Factor X" when you need it is to enter the exam, not in the hope that you might just do enough to slip past the sentries, but with the express purpose of *claiming* the 2,i or first that is rightfully yours. Open a can of 'whup-ass' on the exam, as the Americans would say.

Negative identifiers

Most of the negative identifiers I included in my list on page 131 are defined in opposition to the positive identifiers I have just been discussing, and do not require further explication here. However, there are two negative identifiers that should be considered in their own right. The first, the plot-driven script, is more or less specific to English (and possibly History) essays.

Plot-driven answers

In these sorts of papers the argument seems dictated to by the plot of the novel or play under consideration. Such essays seldom do well. In an examiner's eyes, good students should be able to step outside a plot (or a sequence of historical events) to consider larger issues – that is, those not directly concerned with what happens to whom, and in which order. For instance, let's imagine someone has chosen to write on the Fool in Shakespeare's *King Lear*. This character is the key to a number of intriguing discussions and an able student would want to use him to open a few doors. A less confident student, on the other hand, might be more preoccupied with what the Fool said to Gloucester, what Gloucester said back, and so on. This is dangerous ground: metaphorically speaking, you are standing on the near bank of the river Styx, where a bloke called Charon is offering to ferry you across to the other side for a small fee.

Paraphrase

Paraphrase is when you merely tell the story in your own words, perhaps without realizing that this is what you are doing. Once this happens (to continue the metaphor), you are already floating down the river, wondering why it got so dark all of a sudden.

Paraphrase is a sure identifier of weak work. Desperate students, who can do no more with a text than relate what happens in it, often try to present paraphrase as argument, but examiners are never fooled. If you have a legitimate reason for telling the story (perhaps you are comparing two slightly different editions of a novel, clarifying some problematic aspect of plot, or providing a brief summary of a little-known novel), then make absolutely sure your reader knows what this reason is. Otherwise it will be assumed that you are floundering and trying to find ways to fill the page. Sooner doodle across your script than resort to paraphrase.

Final words

I've never forgotten the advice my old English professor gave me when I was an undergraduate. He said that writing exam essays was a lot like playing cricket. You have to make a choice between two types of stroke. Either you play a firm defensive shot to avoid being bowled out, in which case the best you can hope for is a solid 2,i mark. Or you play the haymaker. Going for the haymaker involves taking an almighty swing at the ball. If you miss (and that's the danger with this kind of shot), you'll overbalance and fall flat on your face, and everyone will laugh. But if you make contact . . .

In other words, nothing ventured, nothing gained. *Carpe diem*, seize the day! Don't be afraid to take risks. Remember, fortune favours the brave!

Above all HAVE FUN! It's only an exam.

Note:

1 Think about preparation: **how** you revise is as important as **what** you revise.
2 Include **positive identifiers** in your work.
3 In an examination **you can be anybody you like**: masquerade as a first-class student, and you might just end up with a first-class mark.

Index